Critical Acclaim for *Got,*

Got, Not Got: The A-Z of Lost Football Culture, Treasures & Pleasures

"A veritable Dundee cake of a book."
Danny Kelly, talkSport

"Recalling a more innocent time before Sky Sports and millionaire players, *Got, Not Got* is like a long
soak in a warm bath of football nostalgia: an A-Z of memorabilia, ephemera and ill-advised haircuts."
In Demand, *Mail on Sunday Live* magazine

"The real magic is the collection and display of the illustrative material of stickers, badges, programme
covers, Subbuteo figures and other ephemera. It is astonishingly thorough, well-presented, inspired
and indeed had me going, 'yes, got, got, not got, forgot, never seen'."
When Saturday Comes

"A cracking book which whisks you back to a different footballing era."
Brian Reade, Mirror Football

"This memorabilia fest is a delightful reminder of what's gone from the game: 'magic sponges',
Subbuteo and, er, magazines for shinpads. Such innocent times, eh?"
FourFourTwo

"The book's great fun. It's an essential if you grew up watching football in the 60s, 70s or 80s.
It's a kind of football fan's catnip. Nobody can quite walk past it. They start looking at it and then
realise they've got something else they should be doing 10 or 15 minutes later."
Paul Hawksbee, talkSport.

"The best book about football written in the last 20 years."
Bill Borrows, *Esquire*

"A body of work that transcends being 'just a book' by a considerable distance."
In Bed With Maradona blog

"Obviously, everybody over the age of 40 is going to absolutely love this.
There's something for every fan of every club."
Andy Jacobs, talkSport

"Browsable for hours, even days, preferably with your favourite records from the 1970s in the
background, this is the Christmas present that every football fan of a certain age yearns to peruse
while their neglected partner's busy basting the turkey and getting quietly pickled on cooking sherry...
Sit back and be blissfully reminded of adverts, food products, players, toys, kits, magazines, stickers
and trends you'd long since confined to your mental attic."
Ian Plenderleith, Stay-at-Home Indie Pop blog

"I've had this for a month but haven't got round to reviewing it because it keeps disappearing.
It's the sign of a good book that people repeatedly pick it up and walk away with it.
A hardback collection of vintage football memorabilia that you need in your life...
It's like finding your old football stickers."
James Brown, SabotageTimes.com

GOT, NOT GOT
The Lost World of Leeds United

Derek Hammond & Gary Silke

Pitch Publishing Ltd
A2 Yeoman Gate
Yeoman Way
Durrington
BN13 3QZ

Email: info@pitchpublishing.co.uk
Web: www.pitchpublishing.co.uk

First published by Pitch Publishing 2013
Text © 2013 Derek Hammond and Gary Silke

13-digit ISBN: 9781909178731
Design and typesetting by Olner Pro Sport Media.
Printed in the UK by CPI Group (UK), Croydon CR0 4YY

"To say that Leeds are playing with Southampton is the understatement of the season. Poor old Southampton just don't know what day it is. Every man jack of this Leeds side is now turning it on – oh, look at that! It's almost cruel. The Elland Road crowd are lapping this up. One has to feel sympathy for Southampton, but the gap between their position and Leeds is an almighty chasm."

Barry Davies, BBC TV *Match of the Day*

*"I remember David coming in the day his pet monkey committed suicide.
It had put its head in the oven.
He was crying his eyes out and, of course, we burst out laughing."*

Gary Sprake

Johnny Giles
INSIDE LEFT

PAUL REANEY
LEEDS

Eddie Gray
OUTSIDE LEFT

PAUL MADELEY
WING HALF

A&BC AND TOPPS

A&BC Chewing Gum of Romford, Essex, holds a special place in the hearts of millions of big kids. Back in the 1950s, it was Douglas Coakley (the 'C' in the company name) who came up with the idea of packaging football cards with a thin slab of chewy, a combination which proved a natural winner. Throughout the 1960s and into the 1970s they produced a yearly set of football cards, as well as other stickers, tattoos and card series covering everything from the Beatles to *Star Trek* – and American sports and TV-related cards bound for the US via partner company, Topps.

Nowadays they're worth anything up to two or three quid each for the 1960s and early Seventies cards in excellent condition – though sadly that price drops off steeply for ones with edges chewed and worn, like ours. The 'crinkle-cut' extra photographs given away free with each pack in 1969 are even more desirable, and the little Action Transfers given away as extras in every pack in 1971 are

worth anything up to seven or eight quid apiece. This for a small piece of paper which was given away in a packet that cost thruppence.

Unfortunately, in 1974, A&BC lost a long-simmering legal battle and was taken over by Topps-Bazooka. End of story.

But, for some reason, it isn't easy to put out of your mind stray memories of football's long-lost people and places, the youthful obsessions and outdated rituals that seemed so important back in the day – and, in a strange way, still do. It might be a name on an email that you immediately associate with a recoloured kit on a card, and think: "Not got." Or just a vacant moment when you're driving at 80mph along the M62, when you find yourself wondering… whatever happened to Rod Belfitt?

It isn't everyone who could possibly understand.

TERRY COOPER
LEEDS UNITED
LEFT BACK

JACK CHARLTON
LEEDS UNITED
CENTRE HALF

LEEDS UNITED

GARY SPRAKE
GOAL-KEEPER

SUBBUTEO

Subbuteo was by far the most popular table-top representation of football, and its '00'-scale figures still hold a special place in the hearts of blokes across the globe. Part of the game's appeal was due to the huge range of accessories which, while unnecessary for the actual playing of the game, did prop up an illusion of realism and 'add to the big-match atmosphere'.

Plastic pitches were one of the ugliest developments in Eighties football. QPR, Luton and Oldham became unbeatable at home because

'Astroturf' pitch – although, if their 'grass' pitch was made of green baize cloth, and the 'Astroturf' surface from slightly different baize cloth, it's unclear in what sense it was any more 'artificial'.

The rampant hooliganism of the time puts into stark perspective any complaints about plastic pitches, leading as it did to football attendances going down and spike-topped fences going up. Subbuteo didn't shirk its remit to mirroring the game and replaced its friendly green picket fences with prison railings and mounted police to keep any

The 'Heavyweights' of the Sixties and Seventies were replaced by Admiral-toting 'Zombies', and then by 'Lightweights'.

they mastered the art of playing on a surface that had all the properties of lino – sliding tackles were out, except for players wearing motorcycle leathers under their shorts. Meanwhile, good old Subbuteo exhibited their usual dogged determination to keep up with the times, producing their own

potential plastic yobboes off the pitch.

The actual Subbuteo playing figures of the late-Sixties to late-Seventies are known these days as Heavyweights, with their National Service haircuts, big white socks and a stance that suggested they were well up for it.

The Seventies also saw short-lived

and unloved 'Scarecrows' and 'Zombies' for the Admiral figures; before the Eighties brought the more detailed, and more popular, 'Lightweights' which endured to the mid-Nineties.

Although accessories such as the dugouts and the ambulance men, the TV tower with mini-Motty, the floodlights and VIP figures (including Queenie handing over a tiny FA Cup) were affordable and always welcome on a Christmas morning, the ultimate prize had to be the Subbuteo stadium, complete with a decent crowd of ready-painted spectators. Unfortunately, they were beyond the pocket of most kids' parents and you'd count yourself lucky to have a single, foot-long stand with a couple of dozen spectators dotted around it.

We used to buy packs of unpainted spectators – fifty per box, all as naked as the day they were moulded – and only after weeks of eye-damaging work on Polo-Neck Man, Fatty, Celebrating Man and his equally Celebrating Girlfriend, did we discover the ultimate irony: with stands on all four sides it was virtually impossible to play the game without nudging a stand and causing a mini-stadium disaster.

Oh, come on, let's go up the park and play football.

Baby Batty:
Butter wouldn't
melt...

"I have a little black book with players' names in it. If I get a chance to do them, I will."

Jack Charlton

The nominated hard man of each club was almost as celebrated as the star strikers they sought to bruise: The bespectacled Norbert Stiles of Manchester United (he had to be hard); Ron 'Chopper' Harris of Chelsea; Liverpool's Tommy Smith, 'The Anfield Iron'; Tottenham's Dave Mackay.

In other words, players you loved to hate – unless they happened to be on your side, in which case there was often room for a small amount of give-and-take. A healthy alternative perspective on their tendency towards ultraviolence.

Take Jackie Charlton, for example: he was a warrior, a loyal servant for 21 years, a man you'd want to go to war with, but certainly not against.

Oppo fans were often incensed by his high spirits, his tenacious, uncompromising tackling and never-say-die attitude, which was totally different in nature to the common yobs previously mentioned. And Norman Hunter, too, was a much misunderstood character.

THE TENACIOUS WARRIOR

1966 is remembered for glorious, golden images of a grinning, red-shirted Bobby Moore, carried on his team-mates' shoulders, holding aloft the Jules Rimet trophy. However, from a non-English point of view, the tournament saw world football reach a nadir of cynical foul play. It's known across the footballing globe as the 'Dirty World Cup'.

It was a time when defenders appeared to have free rein to hoof lumps out of strikers, who were given virtually no protection from referees. Full-backs had grown tired of being made to look like monkeys by the likes of Stanley Matthews and had discovered that there was more than one way to stop a tricky winger.

There seemed to be a complicit understanding between a good old-fashioned hard man and referee whereby no one could be booked in the opening five minutes of a game. He was allowed one free, 'welcoming' clog on an opposing forward's calf, 'just to let them know I'm here'.

The second, Achilles-crunching challenge might warrant a brief word of warning from the ref. The third might occasionally earn a booking, at which the defender would present a picture of outraged innocence.

By this stage, the talented striker had completely lost:

1 – stomach for the contest; or,
2 – all feeling below the waist.

And the job was a good 'un.

DENIM JACKET PATCHES

Back in the day, no self-respecting teenager would be seen at a football match or out on the town without a denim jacket rendered almost invisible under the weight of Coffer sew-on patches down the back and arms.

Leeds Ace in the Pack!
Leeds United Rule OK!

The very sight of these vintage 1970s patches is almost enough to make anybody start nagging their mum to stitch as many as humanly possible on to their parka sleeves and Army Surplus schoolbag.

Back in the day, it was possible for an optimally patched jean jacket to actually double in weight compared to the boring all-blue version bought off the peg.

I'M A LEEDS NUT, indeed. LEEDS UNITED TURN ME ON.

Wahey!

Saturday 6 May, 1972:
'Sniffer' puts Leeds ahead in the 53rd minute...

Founded: 1920. Ground: Elland Road. Manager: Jimmy Armfield. League Champions: 1969, 1974. F. A. Cup: 1972. League Cup: 1968. Fairs Cup: 1968, 1971.

LEEDS UNITED

eds United AFC

THE WONDERFUL WORLD OF SOCCER STARS

How many sets of football cards and stickers do you reckon might have been pushed out into the UK market to mark the occasion of the 1966 World Cup? Ten? Twenty? The answer, you might be surprised to hear, is none. Not a one. Zero.

In recent years a limited test production of A&BC World Cup stamps has emerged, but these are priceless rarities that had no real impact. Even though pocket-size cardboard football cards had been successfully covering the domestic game since the end of the '50s, and European and South American manufacturers had produced trailblazing sticker books for the 1962 finals, it simply didn't occur to anyone to build on these trends.

It was only when England secured Monsieur Rimet's small gold trophy that the enthusiasm really rocketed, kick-starting the British football industry in the stands, in the shops and in sticker albums up and down the country.

In the second half of the '60s, playgrounds rocked to the tribal rhythm of "Got, got, got, got, not got" as kids flicked through their teetering piles in search of that elusive Albert Johanneson, perfectly willing to exchange 200 swaps to fill in the one remaining square left on their checklist.

If us Brits were slow off the mark seeing the possibilities in the market for cards and World Cups, it took even

LEEDS UNITED F. C.

ROD BELFITT

BILLY BREMNER

JACKIE CHARLTON

TERRY COOPER

JOHNNY GILES

EDDIE GRAY

JIMMY GREENHOFF

14

PAUL MADELEY

MIKE O'GRADY

PAUL REANEY

Cup: 1972. L
Cup: 1968. Fairs Cup:
1971.

BILLY BREMNER

FRANKIE GRAY

longer to get the ball rolling on the Euro-led non-sticky sticker front.

In 1967, FKS's *Wonderful World of Soccer Stars* rolled into limited, regional production, reflecting a Golden Age when all you needed to start up business in the football sticker market was a picture deal with an agency – no worries if the images were a season or two out of date, that's what retouching brushes are for – and a distribution deal around the corner shops of Britain.

The idea took off, and 1968 saw the first widely available sticker set, largely repeating the previous year's mugshot efforts. The following season's largely accidental mix of action shots and head-and-shoulders upped the excitement greatly and has rarely been bettered, still offering a real window into the Wonderful, and sadly Lost World of Football in the Sixties.

The business model was clear. Give any football-mad child a packet of (not really very accurately titled) stickers, an album and a pot of Gloy gum, let him stick his first sticker into the allotted slot, surrounded by another dozen blank spaces taunting him, and let nature take its course...

LEEDS UNITED

Founded: 1920
Ground: Elland Road
Attendance record: 57,892
Manager: Don Revie
League Champions: 1969
F.A. Cup Winners: Nil
League Cup Winners: 1968

MICK BATES

ROD BELFITT

BILLY BREMNER

JACKIE CHARLTON

ALLAN CLARKE

TERRY COOPER

JOHNNY 1GLES

15

ACTION MAN

They don't make boys' toys like Action Man any more.

Kids aren't interested in peering through the back of a plastic doll's head and into his 'Eagle Eye' when the maximum thrill available is a slightly blurred view of the back garden. And as for realistic hair and gripping hands... they tend to pall into insignificance next to the Xbox's 3-D virtual world, where it's perfectly possible to drop in on Berlin in 1945 or

They don't make boys' toys like Action Man any more.

you had one Action Man or 22, there just wasn't a game you could base around his non-existent ball skills. The specific types of 'action' mastered by 'the movable fighting man' were limited to bending at the joints and being blown into the air. There was only so much fun you could have dressing a doll in football kit, especially as it exposed his shattered-looking kneecaps. The final straw was the orthopaedic stand which he needed to balance on one leg, hovering over the ball in a sorry personification of inaction.

Because most Action Man enthusiasts kept their figures strictly military, the scarcity value of the football range has more recently seen eBay prices soaring. An original 1960s Leeds kit recently sold on the auction site for £300, and the blue-and-white Action Man team badge given away with the original kit pack can sell for over fifty quid alone. If only you'd kept them, Action Man's two-inch-long white socks could now pay for a decent night out.

Pluto in the year 4567, shredding Nazis and aliens alike with a sonic fire ray akin to a red-mist glare from Norman Hunter.

They'd call Action Man un-PC now – an eight-inch multi-skilled terrorist who thought nothing of changing out of his Nazi Stormtrooper uniform into that of a Navy frogman, a Canadian Mountie or an astronaut. And so into his Leeds United kit for a kickaround with your sister's Barbie in goal.

Unfortunately, that's when our vicious little accomplice became a complete bore. Whether

Try painting Admiral logos down the arms of a bloke
only two inches high.

AIRFIX

Ever since 1955, when they released their 1/72 Spitfire model kit, Airfix had been satisfying little boys' unquenchable thirst for recreating World War II.

You could paint up a boxful of Commandos or Desert Rats and painstakingly put together a Hampden bomber, though how you were supposed to stop the 'cement' from clouding up the glass canopy of the cockpit was anyone's guess.

Even more satisfying than endless war was the 1/32nd scale Airfix Sports Series of Airfix Footballers – your chance to ditch khaki and grey for the far more exciting football colours of white and yellow and blue, and maybe even a few of those other oppo colours.

Up until the mid-Seventies it wasn't too much trouble recreating miniature versions of the kits of the day; but things got a lot trickier after that time.

Go on, you try painting an RFW logo and those yellow and blue pinstripes on the early-Eighties Umbro kit, or a string of electron-microscopic Admiral logos all down the arms of a bloke who's just over two inches tall.

Long boring Sunday afternoons were the perfect time for creating teeny-weeny peacock badges or sock tags – right up until the double misery of *Last of the Summer Wine* and the parental enquiry: "Have you got any homework, son?" reminded you that Monday morning was nearly upon us once again.

Thanks to eBay you can still get that distinctive box through the post with England vs. Germany on the front. Old habits, like old enemies, die hard. And if you've got a steady hand and a couple of hundred hours on your hands, there's no more satisfying way to waste your time.

CHARLES BUCHAN'S FOOTBALL MONTHLY

It was the world's first monthly football magazine, unleashed on Britain's thrill-starved youth in September 1951 – and, despite missing the start of his debut season, Charlie Buchan's proved an instant hit.

Here, at last, was some colour to brighten the grey post-war landscape covered by the monochrome grown-up media. At least, bright pastel colours were daubed over black-and-white photos to vivid effect. And, in an era when kids were only expected to speak when spoken to, Charlie undid the top button of his sports jacket and did his best to address the herberts.

Even from the standpoint of sixty years on, the magazine's format is strikingly familiar, suggesting Charlie's editorial team got it pretty much right first time. There's analysis and tips from ex-pros and other enthusiastic scribblers; there's page-size posters for the bedroom wall, and interviews with players who aren't allowed to say anything.

Thumbing now through Charlie's back pages, he provides a unique window into an unrecognisable world of side partings and V-neck shirts, of rugby boots and weirdly recoloured violet irises.

A strange world of side partings, rugby boots and weirdly recoloured violet irises.

The world's greatest soccer annual: no question what you'll be getting in your stocking this Christmas!

From the magazine's perspective, football was steering into choppy waters when Buchan himself died in 1960, leaving the *Monthly* rudderless in the face of tidal changes such as footballers demanding a minimum wage, and suddenly not all agreeing to sport leather hair.

Although it limped on until 1974, *Football Monthly* never stood a chance against the new generation of marginally more readable comics and magazines put together by people who had heard of the Rolling Stones. *Shoot! Goal.* Mud, even, eventually.

If it proves anything, it's probably that in retrospect every age seems like a Golden Age, provided you were ten.

THE CIGARETTE CARD

In the age of No Smoking – when anyone who fancies a tab is forced to stand outside their office in all weathers, and even crowd into a ramshackle lean-to hurriedly added twixt bar and beer garden – it won't be long until kids don't even recognise the reference to a good old-fashioned gasper, already obscured by the slick, sad euphemism of 'candy stick'.

The sweetie cigarette will soon be no more, like the In-Time Club frequented by Frank Worthington and sundry dancing girls, mud and Don Revie's carpet bowls league.

Sweetie cigarette cards are already an obscurity to kids aged under 20 or 30. And the original pre-war mass cult of the cigarette card proper will soon be nothing but a memory clung to by a disappearing breed of oldsters.

No, not the stout men who smoked for England during the war only to be stamped out underfoot in the fallout from NHS cost-cutting exercises

We posed manfully with a sugary cig dangling from our lips, fooling absolutely everybody.

Back in the day, however, they were clearly the best option for L-plate smokers, both in terms of their unique, chalky-sweet flavour and cunning authenticity, courtesy of a dab of pink food colouring on the burning 'hot' end. And they came with a football card, too, if you were lucky – or a fat cricketer or lady tennis player if the dreaded mixed-sports set was in season.

Barratt's and Bassett's packs of sweet cigarettes were a throwback to the cigarette cards that had died out in the war; but we never realised that at the time. We were too busy posing manfully with our sugary cig dangling from our lips, fooling absolutely everybody.

determined to make everyone live to 200. But us, the jammy-faced kids who remember the contents of Granddad's hand-me-down baccy tin: a length of string (now sneered upon as a throwback to the suspicious, militaristic Scout movement), a penknife (now banned), a Watney's Party Seven can opener ("puncture both sides to ensure even flow"), two shillings and fivepence in assorted, unfamiliar coinage ("Dad, what's a 'farting'?") and a small pack of cig cards in a perished and retied elastic band.

19

"Did anyone see what happened?"
"No, sir. Not us, sir."

PIN-UPS AND COVER STARS

Modestly subtitled 'The World's Greatest Soccer Weekly', *Goal* launched on 16 August 1968, with a right posh do at the Savoy with dolly birds and everything. Well, it was the Sixties.

Its distinctive covers, with a bright yellow title on a red background and circular photo design, owed a nod to pop art, and they've stood the test of time, still looking fresh and bold to this day.

Between those glowing Technicolor covers was a good solid line-up of content, albeit on fairly cheap and rough paper prone to browning with age.

There were vivid posters; features from top players like Bobby Charlton: "Don Revie succeeds by knocking down the opposition. Bill Shankly succeeds by building up his own boys..."; and 'Booter', a Beatle-haired footballer, starred in his own cartoon strip; and we even got to 'Meet the Girl behind the Man', Valerie McKinnon, "who passes the time when Ron of the Rangers is away by doing embroidery."

Goal perhaps became a victim of its own success because exactly a year later,

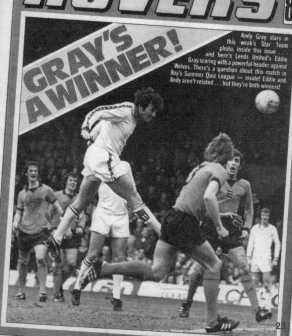

encouraged by decent sales, IPC introduced a second football weekly... entitled *Shoot!*

Better still were the strip-packed comics which also soon emerged, such as *Roy of the Rovers* and *Tiger & Scorcher* and *Score & Roar* and *Scorcher & Score*.

There was nothing again to ever touch that feeling of being blessed by the gods of the pin-up and the cover star – though we'd have to say the cover appearance in *Tiger & Scorcher* was quite a biggie, if you were anything like 10 in 1975!

SUPER COLOUR PHOTO OF ANDY GRAY

ROY OF THE ROVERS 8p

11th JUNE, 1977
EVERY MONDAY

GRAY'S A WINNER!

Andy Gray stars in this week's Star Team photo, inside this issue — and here's Leeds United's Eddie Gray scoring with a powerful header against Wolves. There's a question about this match in Roy's Summer Quiz League — inside! Eddie and Andy aren't related . . . but they're both winners!

South Africa 20c., Australia 30c., New Zealand 30c., Malaysia $1.00.

23

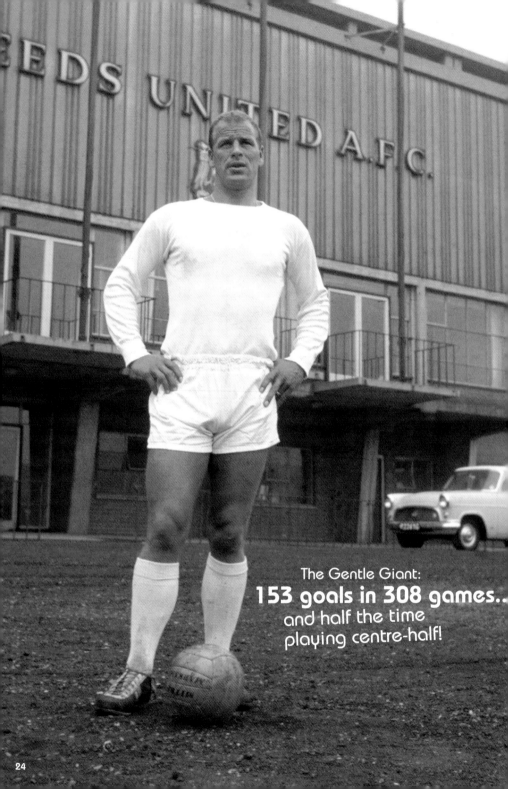

The Gentle Giant:
153 goals in 308 games..
and half the time
playing centre-half!

COTTON

It's the sensual associations that come bundled with cotton that make it such a rich source of minor, if largely subconscious, pleasure.

Ahh, the smell of a new cotton T-shirt being pulled on over your head on a Friday night. The slow fade of a favourite shirt, laundered a hundred times by your mum. Cotton next to the skin – warm against the winter cold, cool in summer... the pure smell of white like pure driven snow, and no labels or logos smelling of a modern attempt to cash in.

In 150 years, the only negatives against cotton were an association with hippie cheesecloth and, ah yes, the institutionalised horrors of the slave trade.

Cotton isn't just perfect for clothes because it's easy to take care of and to wash. It's soft because it's made out of perfectly natural fluff. And it's cheap because the fluff grows on trees.

And so some tiresome bean counter inevitably decided to put about the idea that cotton is altogether second rate. Wear it for sports and it apparently now soaks up sweat in a way that you wouldn't want it to be soaked up. Cotton isn't stretchy enough, and it needs ironing, unlike a certain artificial wonder-fabric. They even tried to convince us that shell-suit bottoms were cooler and more comfortable than jeans.

Now, it just so happens that while cotton is cheap, polyester is cheaper. So much cheaper, it's practically free.

Polyester is an artificial plastic made from the acids and alcohol produced when you torch petroleum – in other words, from exhaust fumes.

Polyester is hard-wearing primarily because it's hard. It's rough to the touch, keeps you cold in winter and hot in summer. Wear it in summer, or for sports, and it will make you smell like you've been dead for a week.

Bring back cotton football shirts!

Yebuggah! Unforgettable Player of the Year in 1995-96, when he also won *Match of the Day*'s Goal of the Season.

BOBBLEHEADS?

We're too old to fully appreciate the glory and power of the so-called 'Bobblehead'.

The Corinthian statuette stands about two inches tall, collecting dust on your shelf, until you've got all 400 of the Whites players ever thus rendered in plastic – at a cost of about 1,000 quid – until such time that you decide to get rid on eBay and make yourself some money out of your hobby of these past 10 years.

Bobbleheads?
We quite like the old ones.

One big job lot should do the trick!

And, sure enough, you raise more than enough readies for a round of drinks at city-centre prices.

That said, this little Gary Speed is enough to make a grown man sigh.

3/2/7? DAVID HARVEY
(LEEDS-UTD)

THE AUTOGRAPH BOOK

Gone out of existence. Withdrawn from the field. Abandoned. Missed. Passed by.

Everything we come across on this journey through the Lost World of Leeds United is no more. They thought it was all over – and they were dead right.

The autograph book was unlike any other of its day. Its cartridge-paper pages were blank, devoid of words and lines, with the built-in compensation of alternate pastel shades – chalky blue, green, pink, yellow. The outer corners of the pages were missing, rounded off so as

The kind of players whose message you'd want to treasure forever.

not to offend the hand of an honoured victim. The spine of the leather-bound booklet ran down the short side, so it lolled open invitingly. On the cover of the book there was no author's name or title, just a single, golden word in a curly typeface. And then there was the vital loop of elastic to hold the book closed in the owner's back pocket, either encircling the whole precious volume, or just stretching over a single corner.

Lost. Let slip. No longer in our possession.

It isn't just the autograph book that has bitten the dust in recent years, but also the crowd

of small boys hanging around the locked double door marked PLAYERS AND OFFICIALS ONLY an hour after the match. The players are missing, too: men who didn't need a minder at their side to talk to a twelve-year-old about the afternoon's brawls and cannonballs. The kind of players whose personally signed message you'd want to treasure forever. Eddie Gray. Carl Harris. Duncan McKenzie. Ray Hankin...

The warning signs came when first two, then three, and now four of the five attackers in every team were phased out, goalscoring deemed surplus to requirement. Local heroes fell out of fashion. Red-faced stoppers failed to evolve with changing times, and so soon became extinct. And the best player in every team of the Sixties and Seventies became the first called up to the great kickaround in the sky.

All gone, but not forgotten.

Then as now, football magazines and club shops churned out sheets of pre-printed (quite literally auto-) autographs to help save the all-important stars time and hassle. It's all a question of supply and demand, see? But it's odd how much more charming the old sheets seem in comparison to today's handily pre-signed official postcards.

BAB

The BAB Souvenir Company was known for just two, instantly recognisable products:

1 The lairy, you might say imaginatively, coloured football club crest sticker.
2 The star-player sticker, always carefully labelled in case of any doubt as to who was depicted.

The modern-day attraction to collectors is essentially down to the fact that, in the early Seventies, hundreds of thousands of children simply couldn't resist unpeeling the backs of the stickers and attaching them to their school bags, school desks, bedroom walls and younger siblings, testing to the limit the proud boast on the retail cards:

Sticks to any surface!
Adidas bags, bedroom walls, younger siblings...

"GREAT! Collect ALL these football 'club' badges," shouted the old counter box. "Sticks to almost any surface."

It could almost have been a long-term strategy to boost values to collectors.

And then there's the sloppy way the company continually recycled their few sticker designs in new and unlikely colours, with endless minor variations, which appeals to the obsessive modern collector.

Admittedly, we mainly like them because they're funny. Is that the spookiest image of 'Sniffer' Clarke you ever did see? Billy Bremner is doing his best to stifle a snigger – at least, the cute version is. The later one's no felt-pen painting itself!

The second coming:
Sergeant Wilko's victorious army,
plus uninvited panda

29

WILKO THE one?

WILKINSON

Like many Leeds fans I was sceptical about the appointment of Howard Wilkinson as Leeds boss - Visions of Leeds playing high altitude footie immediately came to mind.
Sheff Wed conjure up images of the workmen of Wimbledon rather than the finesse that Elland Road fans (supposedly) like. However several factors point in Wilko's favour....... His appointment breaks the ever line... the Revie regime, which for all it's ... ies and insurmountable achievements

Leeds now in Div 2 ...
competitiveness that it ...
The limitations of play...
tried were surely seen ...
To get out of the second...

FANZINES

Following on from the Seventies' music-led revolutions in DIY publishing, it took a while for football to catch up, but eventually fans took to their cranky old typewriters, hunting and pecking and ker-chinging out their frustrations, and learning all-new reprographic skills along the way.

THE HANGING SHEEP
the independent leeds fanzine.
40p   issue 6
KEEP FIGHTING

NEW "RAGAZZO" ALLESSANDRO CORNERED?
THE SQUARE BALL No 2 £1.00
BUT..
STER CRAZY!
INSIDE- VINTAGE GRAY
THE LEEDS FOOTBALL MAGAZINE

They were tired of hearing 'The Fans' View' expressed second hand in the media, where the final word, the final edit, was always predictably happy and safe. Before the 1980s, every word written about football came from an industry perspective – tapped out by writers who were paid by newspapers, magazines, television companies or club programmes, which were in turn reliant on the FA, the League or the clubs themselves.

It's a tough job, running the back page of a local paper without access to news information, player interviews or pictures.

No such problem for the first wave of fanzine rebels, who offered an all-new diet of uncensored opinion cut with terrace humour, finally putting the majority view of 20,000 regulars above the handful of professionals and hired hands – the chairman, the players, the manager, the gentlemen of the press box – who were just passing through.

Suddenly your familiar old programme seller had a bit of competition on the streets from titles such as *The Square Ball*, *ToEllandBack* and *The Hanging Sheep*.

No matter if they were presented under headlines written using felt-pen, Letraset or John Bull Printing Outfit No. 7: here, for the very first time in print, were negative as well as positive views on our beloved clubs and teams, jokes at our own expense, better jokes at our local rivals' expense, album and gig reviews, stories of away trips, pubs and pies... always pies.

And, somewhere along the way, we discovered it wasn't just the fans in our corner of our ground who felt the same way about all-seater stadiums and ID cards, about the wreckers who came to football to chuck bananas and seats on the pitch, and the wreckers who came bearing calculators. And pies.

THE SQUARE BALL NO 4 £1.00
INSIDE!
WEDDOES, PALE SAINTS
REAL ALE & VINTAGE JACK!
PARTY? WHAT PARTY?!
LEEDS UNITED AFC
STRACH DELIVERS THE GOODS!
THE LEEDS FOOTBALL MAGAZINE

THE FOOTBALL CARD ENGINE

Here's how to transform your humble
pushbike into a revved-up, throbbing
beast of a motorcycle, all too easy to
mistake for a 750cc Norton Commando
(provided you're only listening rather
than looking).

Turning heads, wobbling down the gutter
with a guttural Vrrrrrrrrrrp.

All you need is:

1 One giant pile of football cards;
2 Two clothes pegs;
3 An anti-social desire to terrorise
   your neighbours like those cool
   Hells Angels you've seen on
   Nationwide; and,
4 A tragic disregard for your future
   financial security.

If you've got a teetering pile of
cards, it naturally follows that you've got
an even bigger pile of swaps, collected
up over weeks of frustration while
searching for the two or three you need
for the set.

We recommend you use a Frankie
Gray 'blue-back' from Topps' 1976-77
series. He's got a nice woody thrum.

All you have to do is use
the pegs to secure the cards
on to your bike frame so
they stick a little way into
the spokes. Then push off,
taking note of the unusual
sensation of slight resistance
as you wobble down the
gutter, turning heads with
a guttural, engine-like
Vrrrrrrrrrp.

This way, in one
afternoon you might easily
burn through £100's worth
of future sought-after
collectables at 21st-century
prices. But what the heck.
You're only young once, eh?

THE FOOTBALL LEAGUE REVIEW

Run from the back bedroom of secretary Alan Hardaker's Blackpool bungalow, the Football League was devoted to showing everyone what a big, happy family their 92-member club was. *The Football League Review* was a feelgood customer mag, given away free inside club programmes, where it bolstered many four- or eight-page lower-league efforts.

The *FLR* was conspicuous in its absence from several larger League grounds, where power brokers were already wary of growing League influence.

Gloves are for softies: David Harvey takes his chances on the stinging palm front.

However, in stark comparison to the petty politicking backstabbing golf-clubbing small-minded scrap-metal merchant football-club owners of the 1970s, fans dug the freebies to bits – especially if Terry Cooper featured on the cover.

The *Review* was 5 pence 'when bought separately'; which is to say never. It was full of behind-the-scenes peeks at the day-to-day running of all the League clubs, an article on the bootroom at Barrow being just as likely as a visit to the Arsenal trophy room. Then and now, its allure was almost entirely down to staff photographer Peter Robinson, who spent whole seasons travelling around snapping mascots at Mansfield and tea-ladies in Tranmere, thinking up ever more unusual formations for his teamgroups.

"I was conscious that I was different when I talked with other photographers at games," he told

A Frankenstein's monster
of a football sticker...

When Saturday Comes. Robinson never missed an angle, an expression, an oddity or a location, showing more interest in football culture than the game itself. "I felt that you didn't just have to start photographing when the ref blew his whistle. I was interested in the whole build-up to the game."

HASTILY RECOLOURED KIT
Although there was a lot less movement in the transfer market than today, the photo agencies that supplied the football card and sticker manufacturers in the Sixties and Seventies were rarely bang up-to-date.

Cue the burning of midnight oil as heads were snipped off and reapplied to new teammates' bodies, and old shirts hastily penned with new colours.

FKS albums even carried a straight-faced 'guarantee': 'In order to maintain authenticity, some of the players have been photographed in clothing which is not necessarily their official club colours'.

But the filthiest trick in the sticker book has to be the unnatural horror of the head transplant.

For the FKS 1969-70 album, an unsuspecting Johnny Giles was beheaded by the artist (or 'card sharp' in prison slang) who then stuck Coventry's Dietmar Bruck's head onto the Irishman's body in a disgraceful display of deceit and inappropriate forwardness.

The result of this unholy act: a Frankenstein's monster of a football card – and reversing the image and colouring in the grass didn't fool us either.

Look closely,
and you can still make out
Sniffer's Leicester badge
and stripy collar...

ITV SUNDAY AFTERNOON FOOTBALL

Ba ba-ba ba-ba BA-BA BA-BA!

Remember the theme tune from Sunday afternoon football on Yorkshire TV – *Sunday Sport* which became *Football Special* and then *The Big Game*, first presented by Keith Macklin and then Martin Tyler? It must bring back millions of mass memories of roast beef and Yorkshire puddings for the endless trail of nostalgic types who give it a spin on YouTube. It's called 'Sporting Highlights' by easy-listening/TV theme legend Keith Mansfield.

There was little room for manoeuvre in the editing suite,

Remember the theme tune from YTV's *The Big Game?*

back then. The main game, however incident-packed or dull, ran for fifteen minutes up to a half-time ad break, followed by another quarter of an hour for the second half.

Part three brought fifteen minutes of a game from another ITV region. Hugh Johns was the smoky voice of ATV's *Star Soccer*, Tyne Tees was

Kenneth Wolstenholme on *Shoot*, Granada had Gerald Sinstadt on *Kick Off*, while LWT's *The Big Match* was fronted by Brian Moore...

After part four's brief highlights of another game – maybe Norwich or Ipswich from Anglia's *Match of the Week* with Gerry Harrison – and a round-up of results, the weekend seemed almost over.

Dozens of games went untelevised every weekend and that's why seeing your team was so special. With perhaps only a handful of TV appearances in a lean year, the novelty never wore off.

Which is why Whites fans lucky enough to work from home are always sneaking off to YouTube to find clips from the actual matches.

Ba ba-ba ba-ba BA-BA BA-BA!

JAM JAR LIDS

Hartley's Strawberry Jam was already yummy enough, without them coming up with a further incentive for us to consume it even more greedily.

The introduction of footballers' faces to the lids during the 1971-72 season was marketing genius: Billy Bremner, Geoff Hurst, Bobby Moore, Martin Peters, Alan Ball, Gordon Banks, Colin Bell, George Best, Bobby Charlton, Ron Davies, Jimmy Johnstone and Peter Osgood. A stellar line-up of football stars; twelve jars' worth to collect. That was a lot of jam – and a major expense for parents watching every half a new pee – but we ploughed through it somehow.

A 'jam samwich' was one of the few culinary treats you could prepare without parental guidance, and the more you slapped between the slices the nearer you were to your next fantastic lid.

The more jam you slapped between your slices of bread
the nearer you were to your next fantastic lid.

And if you were too full of Mother's Pride or Hovis for another sandwich but couldn't wait to get your hands on the Billy Bremner lid, you could always dip a spoon in and steal a couple more inches... nom nom nom.

I-SPY

Did anybody else out there used to be a 'Redskin' in a previous life – a member of that strange infant cult of I-Spy, where you sent off for membership packs to 'Big Chief I-Spy' at Wigwam-by-the-Water (London EC4)?

The idea was to keep kids occupied, though quite how they would have fared following Big Chief's instructions to the letter is anybody's guess. In the football edition of I-Spy he asked us to nose around our local football ground: did anybody actually try out any of these box-ticking fact-finding missions at Elland Road, where the wrath of club officials would surely have been incurred within seconds:

What else did you notice in the treatment room you saw? ... Score 80.

Which team have you watched

What else did you notice in the changing room you saw? ... Score 80.

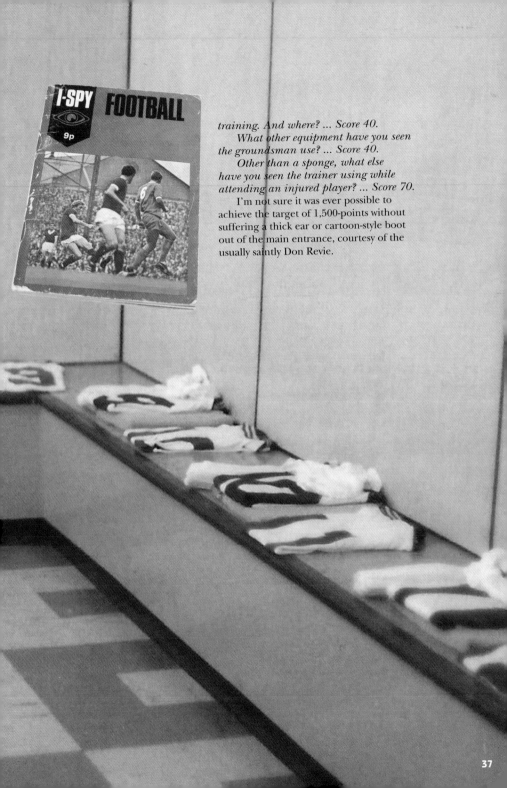

training. And where? ... Score 40.

What other equipment have you seen the groundsman use? ... Score 40.

Other than a sponge, what else have you seen the trainer using while attending an injured player? ... Score 70.

I'm not sure it was ever possible to achieve the target of 1,500-points without suffering a thick ear or cartoon-style boot out of the main entrance, courtesy of the usually saintly Don Revie.

LEAGUE LADDERS

Wahey! Leeds United top of the League!

But there was more to your youthful flights of league ladder-related fantasy than mere self-centred feelgood relish. There was also the bottom of Scottish League Division Two to consider (or maybe, if you were feeling generous, the bottom of the fourth division, and the basement trapdoor beckoning into non-League Hell). That's where a good old English emotion known as *schadenfreude* took over – and where you found clustered the likes of Manchester United, Liverpool, the Sheffield clubs and Bradford City. Not to mention every other side that had put one over on the Mighty Whites in the past three seasons.

Gifted to us in the build-up to the season's big kick-off by *Shoot!* or *Roy of the Rovers* or one of the old-school shoot-'em-up comics such as *Lion* or *Valiant*, the empty league ladders came first, closely followed over a number of weeks with the small cardboard team tabs designed to be poked into their ever-changing slot in the scheme of things.

In the days before computers, even before Teletext, the appeal of being able to stare at the league table was considerable. But, after the third or fourth week, updating your league ladders became a bit too much like hard work.

And that's when you could see what it would look like if East Fife were somehow suddenly transported to second in the League behind its natural eternal leaders. Ha! Swansea in the First Division, and Burnley in the Fourth! And all those lesser Yorkshire clubs mysteriously close to going out of business – pointless, crowdless and hopeless, as God intended.

LEEDS

Ground: Elland Road, Leeds 11.

Team tab: Cut out and keep, and collect the whole set of 92!

the new

1st DIVISION

English League

SHOOT/G

	1st DIVISION		2nd D
1	LEEDS	1	
2	QUEEN'S P. R.	2	
3	SUNDERLAND	3	
4	ASTON VILLA	4	
5	IPSWICH	5	
6	ARSENAL	6	
7	WEST HAM	7	
8	EVERTON	8	
9	DERBY	9	
10	STOKE	10	
11	LEICESTER	11	
12	NEWCASTLE	12	
13	WEST BROM	13	
14	NORWICH	14	
15	BIRMINGHAM	15	
16	COVENTRY	16	
17	MIDDLESBRO'	17	
18	WOLVES	18	
19	TOTTENHAM	19	
20	MANCHESTER C.	20	
21	LIVERPOOL	21	
22	MANCHESTER U.	22	

SOCCER W

Know   ere is to know   OOT. Every
week   informative
articl
gam   tion photograp
          and team

REAT ISS
o"—Nobb   some of Eng
               ns in   in full colour,
The Si   European Cup.
               tion of

n the know-1-

RS

LEAGUE
2nd DIV

	ST. JOHNSTONE
	E. STIRLING
3	MORTON
4	HAMILTON A.
5	STRANRAER
6	ARBROATH
7	ALBION R.
8	COWDENBEATH
	ALLOA
	STIRLING A.
11	EAST FIFE
	DUMBARTON
13	AYR U.
14	QUEEN'S PARK

PROGRESS CHAR

Position	1976																		
	AUG			SEP				OCT				NOV				DEC			JAN	F
	14	21	28	4	11	18	25	2	9	16	23	30	6	13	20	27	4	11	18	25	1	8	15	22	29	5	12
1																									39		
2																											
3																											
4																											

MIRRORCARDS

Back in the sunny 1971-72 season, the *Daily Mirror* was kind enough to give away a set of football cards featuring teamgroups of all 92 League clubs, plus the four Home International squads. The cards could be collected up and stuck on a large wallchart entitled 'Bobby Moore's Gallery of Soccer Sides'.

As if that weren't enough, it was then possible to order from the newspaper's HQ a special giant-size 'My Club' card to take pride of place in the middle of the poster.

The big 'My Club' card
is one of the rarest around.

To be frank, few punters made it this far down the line – making the Leeds United 'My Club' card (not to mention that of some of the smaller third and fourth division teams) one of the rarest around. Especially in mint condition, as those that were ordered were almost inevitably slapped straight on to Junior's wall!

MY CLUB

Leeds United

Back row (l. to r.) : Belfitt, Hunter, Sprake, Harvey, Jordan and Yorath.
Centre row (l. to r.) : Faulkner, Galvin, Jones, Madeley, Clarke and Charlton.
Seated row (l. to r.) : Reaney, Bates, Lorimer, Giles, Bremner, Davey and Cooper.

The *Father Ted* perspective challenge: the small card is big and the big card is far away.

9

STAR SC

SERIES O

Buy the

regularly t

your serie

MIRRORCARD

S
ED

SIDES

lete

Back row (*l. to r.*): Belfitt, Hunter, Sprake, Harvey, Jordan, and Yorath.
Centre row (*l. to r.*): Faulkner, Galvin, Jones, Madeley, Clarke and Charlton.
Seated row (*l. to r.*) : Reaney, Bates, Lorimer, Giles, Bremner, Davey and Cooper.

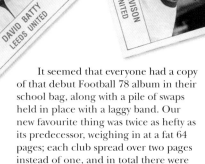

PANINI

Panini's first set of domestic League cards came out under the Top Sellers name in 1972, but it wasn't until later in the '70s that they hit their stride, producing uniform, trusted sticker sets which were actually sticky.

Under this onslaught, A&BC lost their way and were bought out by the American firm Topps, who temporarily brought a little baseball card razamatazz and glam-rock style to proceedings. Still, the days of cardboard were numbered – as were those of good old FKS, who responded to the Panini steamroller with their own sticky set of bizarre gold stickers in 1978 before quietly biting the dust.

The Panini Revolution stood for reliability, professionalism, mass popularity and a return to hundreds of near-identical head shots, albeit with little flags and team crests.

It seemed that everyone had a copy of that debut Football 78 album in their school bag, along with a pile of swaps held in place with a laggy band. Our new favourite thing was twice as hefty as its predecessor, weighing in at a fat 64 pages; each club spread over two pages instead of one, and in total there were 525 stickers to collect.

The stickers themselves were beautifully designed, clear head-and-shoulders shots with a club badge and a flag of St. George or St. Andrew because, yes, the Scots had been included too. Clydebank's Billy McColl got to have his own sticker, and the English Second Division was also covered with a team group and badge for each previously ignored team.

Ah, those badges. There was a heartbeat jump when you ripped open your packet and saw a gold foil United badge nestling among the half-dozen stickers...

Midfield. Born Port Talbot. Ht.5.3½ Wt.9.0. Age 24. Made his name with his first club, Burnley, where he made over 100 League appearances before transferring to Leeds in October 1977. Made his debut for Leeds against Norwich in November 1977, and is an automatic first team choice. ●26,●1(W).

Midfield. Born Edgware. Ht.5.11.Wt.12.5. Age 29. A brilliant player who turned professional with Watford in May 1967 after short spells with Chelsea and QPR. Made his name with Sheffield United, where he changed from striker to midfield, and moved to Leeds in July 1976 for £250,000. ●12, ●2(E).

Midfield. Born Huddersfield. Ht.5.8½.W Age 30. Cost Leeds £100,000 in June when they bought him from Huddersfi had started there in 1963 as a 15-ye amateur, and has now developed into ular choice for club and country. He reputation as a hard player. ●17(E

JIMMY ARMFIELD (Manager)

DAVID STEWART

PAUL REANEY

RANKIE GRAY

PAUL M

N McQUEEN

TREVOR CHERRY

ALEX SABELLA

LEEDS UNITED

LEE CHAPMAN
LEEDS UNITED

Panini reigned for a good fifteen years, never straying far from their '78 blueprint, producing a series of highly collectable and well-loved albums until they, in turn, were replaced by Merlin around the time the Premier League was launched and the licensing fees leapt up.

The Panini Football 1991 sticker album proudly bore the crests of the Football League and the PFA together with that of the Scottish League and pro body counterparts. What Panini didn't know was that Merlin (AKA good old Topps, if you read the small print) were waiting in the wings to scupper the comfy status quo with a deal already tied up with the brand-new Premier League.

In 1992, Panini's remaining PFA licence allowed them only to produce stickers without club colours or details. How sad it was to see official stats replaced by weedy 'captain's comments' and players trotted out in standard white PFA boiler suits – or else players' kit recoloured in lairy greens, reds and oranges in the utterly emasculated 'Super Players From Top Teams' of '96.

While Panini responded by skittering down the leagues for material, Merlin's Premier League 1994 debut featured PL badges, team groups, full info and players in kits, bright and beautiful. There was even a page for Sky TV cards.

43

Welcome to Elland Road: The Liverpool team coach pulls up tight to the players' entrance.

COFFER SPORTS

catalogue '74/'75

EMBLEM
NORTHAMPTON–LONDON

LEEDS

PRINTED SUPPORTER SCARF
The most popular of scarves. Printed scarves
are made in satin-type material and are
available for virtually all clubs and colours

LEEDS UNITED CHAMPIONS FIRST DIVISION 1969

COFFER

In the days when no item of bling was complete without a little football badge or a cocky slogan, Northampton- and London-based Coffer Sports were the jewellers to a nation of kids. They had a wonderful range of pendants, identity bracelets, rings, sew-on patches, lapel badges and key-rings, all tastefully(ish) crowned with enamel club badges.

"Metal club badges are probably our biggest selling line," Arthur Coffer explained to the *Football League Review* in 1973. "For many fans the collecting of these lapel badges has developed into almost a cult. But rosettes are not far behind. We make more than half a million of them a year, in all sizes and all colours, and I cannot see them losing their appeal even though there are signs that the soccer souvenir market is slowly changing."

Slowly changing? Surely not.

You mean to say it's no longer the case that LEEDS GOTTA LOTTA BOTTLE?

Next to Ali, **LEEDS UTD ARE THE GREATEST**

FOOTBALL ROSETTE — Heart shaped
As more women become interested in foot
we are finding a greater demand for souve
to meet female tastes. This product is
designed for the female football fan, and
an original adaption of the established
football rosette

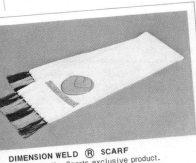

DIMENSION WELD ® SCARF
Another Coffer Sports exclusive product.
Dimension Weld ® football crests are
applied to this 100% orlon scarf providing
a most attractive and popular product.
Most leading teams available.

LADY'S SET
A most attractive exclusive Coffer Sports
product; consisting of a beret and a long
scarf knitted in dog-tooth style for leading
clubs only.

OLYMPIC VEST
Extremely popular as a fashion product for
young people, Coffer Sports have enhanced
this item with a small crest. This vest will
have a double attraction to the young fans
both for fashion and football.
All major teams available.
Sizes: 26" 28" 30" 32" 34".

Give it a vest: Double
attraction for fans of
Leeds United and girls
from 1975.

PETER LORIMER Leeds Utd

LEEDS UNITED & SCOTLAND EXCLUSIVE GOAL ANALYSIS ON PAGE 47

Leeds United

THE BEDROOM SHRINE

You can rebuild it, y'know – the bedroom shrine of your youth when you loved them all, even the dodgy old centre-back on whom the adults had begun to pour scorn and derision.

When you wanted to see their images last thing at night and first thing in the morning; arranged in teamgroup ranks, watching over you while you slept.

The thrill of opening a *Goal*, or *Shoot!* or *Tiger* and seeing a real actual Leeds United hero featured on a colour poster – or, even better, a team photo in the centre spread – might not be so keen now. But don't let that hold you back.

You can still get the horrible woodchip wallpaper we all had in our bedrooms, and paint it that turquoise light blue that was in vogue in the mid-Seventies. Someone will still have the recipe.

And there are people on eBay who make it their business to go through old magazines and annuals pulling out the posters of your club, flogging them by the dozen. The collection that took you seven years to accrue can now be obtained in a couple of days.

It won't have organically spread across your wall over the years like a fungus of devotion, but it will still look magnificent.

Almost certainly, the wife will understand.

TERRY YORATH
Leeds Utd
& Wales

SHOOT/GOAL

SHOOT Presents
LEEDS UNITED
LEEDS UNITED A.F.C.

LEEDS

PAUL MADELEY

LEEDS

TREVOR CHERRY

SHOOT!/GOAL

ALLAN CLARKE Leeds

TEAM SETS | LEEDS UNITED

PAUL MADELEY   GARY SPRAKE   JACK CHARLTON

ALLAN CLARKE   NORMAN HUNTER   MICK JONES

START NOW! COLLECT THE WHOLE SERIES!

SHOOT/GOAL

EDDIE GRAY
LEEDS

MICK JONES
LEEDS UNITED

BRIAN FLYNN
Leeds Utd.

SHOOT!

49

UNITED

White Shirts
White Shorts

Y SPRAKE	1
L REANEY	2
Y COOPER	3
BREMNER	4
CHARLTON	5
N HUNTER	6
O'GRADY	7
N CLARKE	8
CK JONES	9
NNY GILES	10
DIE GRAY	11

TEAMS THAT YOU CAN RECITE

When teams were teams rather than private contractors of fleeting acquaintance, the first-choice line-up would go unchanged for seasons on end, with the boss blooding a kid or adding perhaps one new face over the close season, but only to replace the arthritic right-back who had just enjoyed his testimonial year.

You knew your team was a team because they piled into a team bath after the match, rather than wearing flip-flops and initialled dressing-gowns and insisting on private shower cubicles. You knew they were a team because their surnames seemed to rhyme when you recited them.

Sprake, Reaney, Cooper, Bremner, Charlton, Madeley, Lorimer, Clarke, Jones, Giles, Gray. What's the United team you can automatically recite?

Every year, you'd hear a news story about a fan who had named their firstborn after their whole beloved team. Take a bow, Gareth Paul William John Paul Peter Allan John Edward Blenkinsop. You'll be coming up 43, next birthday. And, of course, it's now a family tradition to name a little one after your heroes, even though it doesn't really work so well in the era of 30-strong Championship squads.

So spare a thought for poor little Patrick Lee Adam Thomas Jason Luke Paul Rodolph Noel Luke Jamie Aidy Stephen Danny Michael Michael David Matt El Hadji Scott Zac Sam Dom Simon Ryan Charlie Chris Alex Ross Alex Ross (sic) Blenkinsop.

'Patsy' for short. Smashing little girl.

LEEDS UNITED

White Shirts, White Shorts

	Mervyn DA
	Mel STERLAN
	Jim BEGL
	Vinnie JON
	Chris FAIRCLOUG
	John McClellan
	Gordon STRACHAN (Ca
	Chris KAMAR
	Lee CHAPMA
	Imre VARA
	Gary SPEE

LEEDS UNITED

White Shirts
White Shorts

GARY SPRAKE	1
PAUL REANEY	2
TERRY COOPER	3
BILLY BREMNER	4
JACKIE CHARLTON	5
NORMAN HUNTER	6
MIKE O'GRADY	7
ALAN CLARKE	8
MICK JONES	9
JOHNNY GILES	10
EDDIE GRAY	11

50 Any alteration to these teams will be

LEEDS UNITED
ALL WHITE

1. SPRAKE, Gary
2. REANEY, Paul
3. COOPER, Terry
4. BREMNER, Billy
5. CHARLTON, Jack
6. HUNTER, Norman
7. GREENHOFF, Jim
8. LORIMER, Peter
9. MADELEY, Paul
10. GILES, Johnny
11. GRAY, Eddie

SQUELCHERS

When it comes to 1970s petrol freebies, many fans of a certain age have their nostalgic favourites. It might be the miniature plastic player busts issued by Cleveland Petroleum in 1971, or the foil club badges that were given away every time dad bought four gallons of Esso 4-star. But it takes a special kind of purist to reserve a missionary zeal for the delights of Esso's set of Squelchers.

These were small, badly bound booklets full of facts of varying degrees of likelihood (and veracity, as it turns out), designed "to squelch arguments about football." Though of course, in pubs and playgrounds all over the country, all they really did was start arguments…

"Squelch!" you were supposed to butt into other people's conversations, fumbling open your blue plastic folder to recite: "Johnny Giles went on record to say, 'Jack Charlton isn't always right, but he's never wrong.'"

There were 16 themed Squelchers in the set. And, even today, it's hard to do without them on a long away trip by rail.

"Don't be silly," you're invited to read aloud as a conversation-starter. "Leeds United came within an ace of winning a 1970 'treble' of League championship, FA Cup and European Cup."

Woe betide any fan who should ever make a factual blunder within your earshot. The chance of a lifetime!

An opportunity to whip out your Squelcher and humble a fellow football fan.

"SQUELCH!" you announce to your brand-new acquaintance in the snug at the notorious Twirling Star public house. "It was Bill Shankly who said in 1969, after the title-clinching 0-0 at Anfield, "Leeds United are worthy champions. They are a great side."

Surely a fitting way to draw to a close any further discussion regarding the finest ever football giveaways. With an all-time classic collectable. And before anyone gets hurt.

"Anyone can score a goal from a penalty"

"Leeds United are worthy champions. They are a great side."

Who said that?

Bob Graham, a newly adopted favourite of the 'Kop'.

Peter Lorimer in action for The Peacocks.

JUMPING OVER MINIS

"I was only sixteen at the time. It was one of those things that kids do," explained Duncan McKenzie to *Leeds United Monthly*.

Well, I don't remember doing it, do you?

McKenzie, born in Grimsby in 1950, played his football when maverick talents were not in short supply; but could Hudson, Worthington or Bowles jump over a Mini?

McKenzie could, and he did so before a game at Elland Road, just to prove it.

For Dunc's next trick...

Telephone
587262

aire le

ZIEBA

He could also throw a golf ball the length of a football pitch, another impressive if ultimately useless achievement.

Having made his name at Nottingham Forest, McKenzie was Brian Clough's first signing as short-lived manager of Leeds. Supporters of Anderlecht, Everton, Chelsea and Blackburn also enjoyed his talents in brief but brilliant helpings. Everton fans still talk about him nutmegging Tommy Smith in a Maine Road semi-final against Liverpool. The Anfield Iron's verdict was: "The best place for Duncan McKenzie is in a circus."

I'd buy a ticket for that.

THE TESTIMONIAL MATCH

When was the last time you went along to pay your respects to a great old servant of your club, putting up with the prospect of a meaningless friendly against big local rivals – it's never quite the same, on their days off – in order to chip in to the loyal clubman's retirement nest egg as he looked forward to living in temporarily reduced circumstances and having to get a proper job? Eh?

There's no such thing as a testimonial match any more. Lining the pockets of a multi-millionaire with the proceeds of a kickaround against a team with the suffix 'XI' doesn't count. The vital elements of long service, need, mutual gratitude and respect are all absent.

Here's the cover of Eddie Gray's testimonial programme in 1979 and the match ticket (which was just £1.50!). It was Eddie Gray's team, which was the current Leeds side at the time versus 'Super Leeds', which included the majority of the Don Revie team.

The game ended up 4-1 to Super Leeds!

ALL THE BEST, EDDIE.

Leeds Utd.
Association Football Club Limited
ELLAND ROAD
LEEDS LS11 0ES

TICKET AND MATCH
INFORMATION
Telephone 0532 702621
(24 hour service)

EDDIE GRAY'S X1 V LEEDS U

TESTIMONIAL   7.30.P.

STAND D   WEST STND   B/A
ROW SEAT
S 224 £1.50   280321

Leeds

Joe Jordan

International Appearances	26
International Goals	7
League ~~...es~~	143
Leag~~...~~	39
He~~...~~	5'11¾"

Leeds Utd

Peter Lorimer

International Appearances	
International Goals	
League Appearances	21
League Goals	4
Height	408
	150
	5'10"

TOP TRUMPS

Kids used to flip their cards at playground walls, either trying to get closest to the bricks or cover the oppo, and of course we jammed millions of pounds' worth of cards into the spokes of our bikes to get a groovily authentic engine noise.

Hence, Top Trumps were invented in the '70s to give card-owning a little more of a competitive dynamic:

Joe Jordan... no way are you getting him off me... unless you have a six-footer... or someone with 40 league goals...

Peter Lorimer... is a bit more susceptible on height and international goals... shame they don't have the category 'Hot Shot MPH: 70'.

This head-to-head game-playing tradition was revived in the mid-'90s by Subbuteo Squads sets, and powers into the future with Shootout cards.

Captured for posterity:
Bad hair day at Elland Road.

Mister Softee issued their '1st Division Football League Club Badges' for the 1971-72 season, featuring the 22 top-flight clubs plus England and Wales... but not Scotland where, presumably, it's a bit chilly for ice cream and lollies.

Rarer editions of this set, which was issued for one more season, were branded 'Lord Neilson' and 'Tonibell'.

Was it just our dads that said: "You know when the chimes are going? That means they've run out of ice cream"?

WE ALL SCREAM FOR ICE CREAM

We're guessing the ice cream industry hasn't had a great time of it recently, given the drizzly nature of our rather rubbish summers (notlikewhenwewerekids). Well, maybe they should start giving football badges away with their ice cream, like they did in 1971. That would soon have us running to the end of the street every time we heard the chimes playing 'The Whistler and his Dog'.

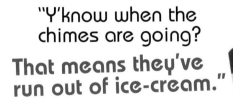

"Y'know when the chimes are going? That means they've run out of ice-cream."

1ST DIVISION FOOTBALL LEAGUE CLUB BADGES

LEEDS UNITED
The three owls found on the Leeds United club badge come from the crest of Sir John Savile, the first alderman of Leeds in 1931. The fleece, shown in the centre of the badge, represents the town's association with the wool industry.

PRESENTED BY
Mister Softee
1971

collect the whole smashing set of **JOE MERCER'S GREAT BRITAIN SQUAD '71**
all 16 Soccer Star Models free from Cleveland

Jimmy Johnstone, Mike England, Bobby Moore, Billy Bremner, Alan Mullery, Terry Cooper, Pat Jennings, George Best, Tommy Gemmell, Gordon Banks, Colin Bell, Ron Davies, Keith Newton, Geoff Hurst

JOE MERCER'S GB SQUAD

Even back in the early Seventies, those corrupt politicking jobsworths at FIFA were making noises about the home countries' historic standing as separate nations in international football (which we just happened to be pretty good at), while England chose to club together with our cousins from the Celtic fringes when it came to doing PE (which we always used to be pretty crap at) in the Olympics.

My, how we smirked when good old Cleveland Petroleum gave Man City boss Joe Mercer free rein to pick his fantasy GB squad, converting his wall picks into small but perfectly formed plastic busts, in the classical tradition.

With the England side still ranked number two in the world behind Brazil (in our minds, at least) after the Mexico World Cup, it took barely any imagination at all to imagine a squad that included Banks, Cooper and Moore (England), Bremner and Johnstone (Scotland), Best and Jennings (Northern Ireland) and Ron Davies (Wales – just go with the flow, okay?) winning the next World Cup for fun.

In retrospect, it seems a bit of a shame we didn't do as FIFA suggested and thrash the blighters fair and square. Lordie knows we had every chance when Mercer became caretaker England boss just three years later, in 1974.

Small but perfectly formed plastic busts, in the classical tradition.

MARSHALL CAVENDISH FOOTBALL HANDBOOK

Long before the age of YouTube or even the ubiquitous video recorder, there was no easy way to replay golden goals from the past – you just had to wait for them to be reshown on *Football Focus*, which could often prove quite a lengthy wait if you were waiting for a specific goal.

At least there was some respite provided by the *Marshall Cavendish Football Handbook* ("in 873 weekly parts") and their smashing arrow- and dot-laded diagrams which traced the build-up to a goal in stunning time-lapse cartoon form.

It was very much as if you were actually there.

Wonder at the Tony Currie triplets as they bamboozle the likes of Baker and Nicholl in the Saints defence before launching a rocket shot past Gennoe from fully half a page.

The Marshall Cavendish arrow-and-dot diagram shows every goal **in stunning ImaginationVision,** complete with added slight confusion!

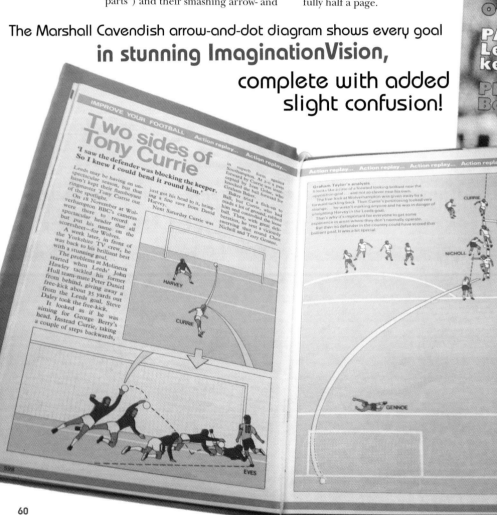

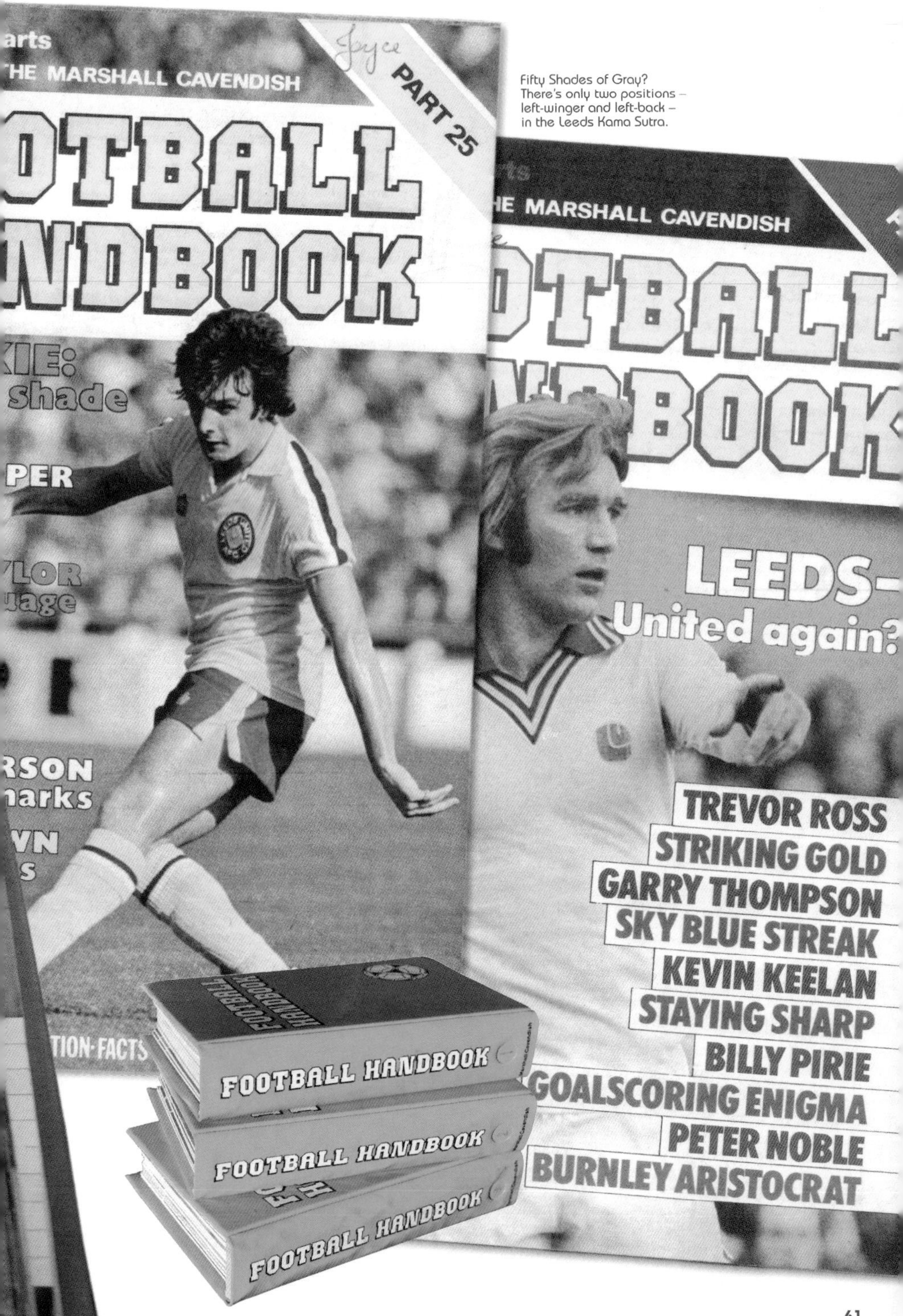

FOOTBALL HANDBOOK

KIE:
shade

PER

YLOR
uage

RSON
marks

WN
s

TION·FACTS

Fifty Shades of Gray?
There's only two positions —
left-winger and left-back —
in the Leeds Kama Sutra.

arts

THE MARSHALL CAVENDISH

FOOTBALL HANDBOOK

LEEDS–
United again?

TREVOR ROSS
STRIKING GOLD
GARRY THOMPSON
SKY BLUE STREAK
KEVIN KEELAN
STAYING SHARP
BILLY PIRIE
GOALSCORING ENIGMA
PETER NOBLE
BURNLEY ARISTOCRAT

FOOTBALL HANDBOOK

FOOTBALL HANDBOOK

FOOTBALL HANDBOOK

FOOTBALL HANDBOOK

"Say Cheese!"

WAGS

England's World Cup Finals campaign of 2006 was unusual not for the team's results but for the size of their entourage. The squad's luggage truck at Frankfurt Airport was weighed down not just by 23 kits, tracksuits and toilet bags, but by equipment belonging to a further 95 backroom staff and specialists, including chiropodists, masseurs, shrinks and warm-up/down/sideways coaches.

Then there were the additional two trucks needed to carry the portable wardrobes, multi-gyms, tanning paraphernalia and bling belonging to the players' wives and girlfriends – the newly coined WAGs.

Compare and contrast with the Leeds players' lovely ladyfolk on their way to the 1970 FA Cup Final. Not a recording contract or book deal between them.

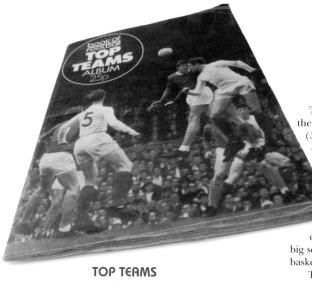

To ensure that you kept buying these weekly parts at a cool 23p (*Shoot!* was only 6p at this time) an extra incentive was nailed on to the deal.

In part two you got this 'Book of Football – Top Teams' album and each week a sheet of 16 'stickers' in random order was issued. After carefully cutting them out with the big scissors from your Mam's sewing basket they were ready to be glued in.

They had you trapped now, for your quid a month.

Only when all your Leeds heroes were present and correct on their page could you relax once more.

TOP TEAMS

In 1971, the good people at Marshall Cavendish, of Old Compton Street, launched their *Book of Football*, a part-work encyclopaedia in 75 issues.

THE RATTLE

The other day, I wandered down to the football from the pub and took my seat at one minute to kick-off, as usual, in order to avoid any kind of 'match-experience' shenanigans. Before I could sit down I had to extricate an object from the laggy band that secured it to my seat. It was a folded sheet of laminated card in club colours, called a 'clap-banner', which explained the horrendous noise that had assaulted my eardrums since I'd entered the ground.

Needless to say, I immediately took against it.

But when the frenzied clacking had died down a bit, I did at least concede that my age was partly to blame. For I once received a football rattle for my birthday that made a quite spectacular noise when I whizzed it round my head. So much so, that its use had to be rationed in the house.

One (young) person's great sound is another (old) person's unholy racket. That explains why the vuvuzela all but ruined the 2010 World Cup for me (along with England's risible performance), while some people thought they were such splendid fun, they started to take them to League games the following season.

The football rattle enjoyed its heyday in the 1960s, when they became as iconic a symbol of football-supporterdom as the scarf and bobble-hat.

They were nearly always homemade, employing the sort of engineering skills that only Dad could manage, and painted up in glossy club colours with the team name added as a finishing touch.

What modern day Health & Safety laws would have to say about spinning a fairly hefty chunk of wood at speed round your head in a tightly packed crowd, I don't know.

"You'll have someone's eye out," probably.

One (young) person's great sound is another (old) person's unholy racket.

MY FIRST SHOOT!

Allowed one comic a week,
I'd already graduated from the
entry-level *Beano* to *Scorcher*,
but not until the summer of
1974, while immersed in the
West Germany World Cup, did I
consider myself man enough to
step up to *Shoot!*

Eight pence was the price of
admission, and I was soon in beyond
the full-colour cover of Billy Bremner
playing for Scotland against Brazil.

Now I could absorb an article by
Bobby Moore; could puzzle over the
fiendish problems posed in 'You Are
the Ref'; study up-close World Cup
action featuring Australia, Scotland,
Holland, Zaire, DDR and Yugoslavia;
chortle at the 'Football Funnies'; 'Focus
On' Paul Gilchrist of Southampton
(Miscellaneous Likes: motor racing, oil
painting, music), and realise there were
people just like me all over the country,
courtesy of the 'Goal Lines' letters page
and 'Ask the Expert' readers' queries.

If I was lucky, there'd be a full-
page star poster to add to my shrine,
though this only happened once in a

KS Tollesley

SHOOT! 8p

1st JUNE, 1974

IN COLOUR INSIDE:
PART ONE OF OUR
SPECIAL PULL-OUT
WORLD CUP 1974
WALLCHART

Australia — 25c.
New Zealand — 25c.
South Africa — 25c.
Rhodesia — 27c. Nigeria
— K.20, Malaysia —
80c, Spain — Pst. 18.
Norway — Kr.2.40,
Sweden — Kr.1.75
Inklmoms, Malta — 7c.9.
Italy — L.300,
Holland — Fl 1.00

EAST GERMANY v.
ENGLAND — by
Bobby Moore

"We Are The Champions!"
Leeds' captain Billy Bremner is
chaired by his team-mates as
he shows the Elland Road fans
the 1973/74 League Championship trophy.

SPOTLIGHT—OUR RECORD OF SEASON 1973-74 BEGINS

WITH JOH

teams future

Allan Clarke (Leeds)

blue moon. It's difficult to explain now how a photo could be so prized, Blu-Tacked instantly up on your wall, but in the days of black newsprint papers and monochrome TV, the eight colour pages in *Shoot!* were like oases in a grey desert.

For five years my collection grew, filling several boxes, until 1979 when my head was finally turned by an attractive newcomer called *Match Weekly*.

I'm sorry I dropped you, *Shoot!,* and I'm even sorrier that we now live in a world where kids can't leg it down to the newsagents to eagerly pore over the latest issue.

67

MOBIL BADGES

We love these silk badges given away with Mobil petrol in the late '70s.

When was the last time you visited a petrol station to be gifted a football collectable that you thought was worth holding on to for 35 years, fer chrissakes?

Made of pure 100% silk from a silkworm's bottom* and, as such, suitable for stitching on to your Sunday best anorak or parka?

Free with four gallons of 4-star.

The only downside, associated more with the free giveaway poster than the patches themselves, was the prospect of a giant Alan Hudson marauding down the country like King Kong or Godzilla or worse – Dribble of Destruction Horror Shock – stomping his way down the country and landing on your delightful suburban semi.

probably not strictly true.

UNITED CHOCOLATE BAR

Like many of the sweets of our
childhood, the United bar is no longer
produced, and is much missed. Crunchy
honeycomb wrapped in chocolate,
in three bite-sized pieces, available in
Original and Orange... I'm actually
salivating right now.

The TV advert from around 1980
reinforced the link with football with a
cartoon cast singing along as they went
to the match.

"My name is Stan, I am a fan,

And I'm delighted, to eat United."

"My name is Stan, I am a fan,
And I'm delighted, to eat United.
We are the fellas, the shouters and
yellers,
And we never miss, this crunchy
candy crisp.
I am the boss, and some things make
me cross,
But even I'm delighted, to eat
United."

Er, we take it these popular snacks
were named after *Leeds* United,
right? There aren't any other serious
alternatives.

Hopefully McVities will bring
back the jewel in the crown of our
school packed lunches – though,
admittedly, this could cause a little
confusion as they are now owned
by United Biscuits.

THE GREEN 'UN

This same ritual went on up and down the
country for decades, little kids and old
blokes queuing up outside the paper shop at
6 o'clock on Saturday night, waiting for the
sports final edition of the local paper – the
Green 'Un, the *Pink 'Un*, the *Blue 'Un*
or the *Buff*. Any colour as long as it wasn't
white. Here was sports journalism at its most
demanding, where reports were phoned in
on the hoof, assumptions were made before
the final whistle, and last-minute goals were
any editor's nightmare.

The *Yorkshire Evening Post Sports
Final* was vital reading for those fans who
couldn't rest until they had read a report
of a game that some of them had seen
eighty minutes ago (unless they were after
confirmation of a result they'd just heard
played out on the radio).

The *Green Post* gave you the chance to
settle down in a favourite armchair, to check
the pools and peruse the results and league
tables at your leisure. In the days before Sky
News and even Ceefax, it was either this or
wait for the arrival of the Sunday papers.

Gradually the need for a Saturday
evening sports edition lessened and then
disappeared altogether. The internet was
one blow – suddenly you didn't need to be
standing out on the street in January – but
the killer was the spreading of fixtures over
the weekend due to the demands of TV.

One by one, the sports papers had to
admit defeat and hold up their hands in
surrender, in Manchester and Liverpool,
Leicester and Coventry and Birmingham...
although the Norwich *Pink 'Un* and
Ipswich's *Green 'Un* are both websites now.
If you can't beat 'em, join 'em.

The great Don Revie
side all arrived
simultaneously in an
advanced state of
football maturity.

View from the stands:
Leeds visit Dean Court,
        Bournemouth, back in 1988.

LUFC

BADGES DEEMED NO LONGER SUITABLE FOR A MODERN, GO-AHEAD CLUB

The history of every club's crest is virtually the same – a tale of tradition overtaken by misguided grooviness overtaken by the branding department.

How easy it used to be to design a striking, classic football club badge back in the early 20th century. The town arms was always a sound starting point, as was the club motto or the admirable beastie associated with the nickname. Often, two or three of the options were combined with timeless elan using the expert skills of the draughtsman and the artist – much to the confusion of the pixellated chumps who now earn too much clicking the Weird filter on Photoshop.

Hats off to the bloke who originally captured the essence of Norman Hunter in a dead, hanging sheep. Plain and simple, the town arms did Leeds fine up until 1960.

And then some joker gave the Peacocks the Owl badge of near-neighbours Sheff Wed, only for it to eventually run up against Don Revie's bizarre superstitious hatred of birds! It was duly replaced with simple 'LUFC' script for a couple of years.

There was true genius behind the 'Smiley' badge, a Seventies icon which lasted right through till 1983 in various forms and borders, until it was unexpectedly replaced by shirt manufacturers Umbro with the stylised peacock badge – a bit odd, really, seeing as how the old nickname wasn't exactly in everyday use.

No worries, mind. The badge would get another redesign in 1984 – the rose and ball – and again in the 90s with Peter Ridsdale's European shield, which remains the basis of the current badge with the little ball and rose reinserted. Must be almost time for another prod, another retexture, another 'freshen up'...

FA CUP CENTENARY COINS

Good old Esso. Every year, they brought out something great for us to collect, and 1972 was no different. The handsome 'FA Cup Centenary 1872-1972' brochure and coin collection was such a must-have item for every young boy that silence must surely have descended on the forecourts of Shell garages while the offer was on, with tumbleweed blowing around between deserted BP, Jet and Cleveland pumps.

There were 30 of these "silver-bright, superbly-minted Centenary Coins" to collect, one per visit to the Esso station, the album to house them in representing a modest Dad Tax of 15p.

But everyone from the Wanderers and Blackburn Olympic through to more recent winners was very nicely trumped and put into the shade a week after the Cup Final – with the minting of the big gold-coloured centrepiece coin, commemorating Leeds' historic Wembley victory over Arsenal.

The big gold centrepiece coin commemorated
Leeds' recent Wembley victory over Arsenal.

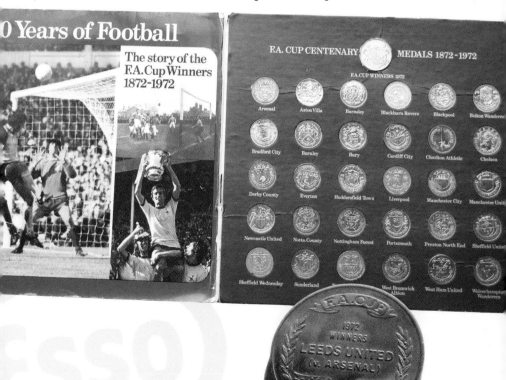

POSING IN YOUR LEEDS GEAR

Here's little Mark Jordan posing in his Admiral away shirt, looking for all the world like namesake Joe.

It was a magic feeling, pulling on your team's shirt, shorts and socks. And then looking down at the badge. It was the kind of occasion that warranted pestering your mother to get the camera out.

"Mam, take it now. Take it while I'm doing this..."

Waiting impatiently between shots while she 'wound it on'.

Standing up with your arms folded, with one foot on the ball, or crouched down holding

MARK JORDAN
LEEDS
MIDFIELD

"Mam, quick, take it now.
Take it while I'm doing this..."

the ball with splayed out fingers... it wasn't your mam anymore, it was the official club photographer on photocall day, taking the photo that would appear in *Shoot!* or on a football card. Or else you were your club's brand new signing, and a gaggle of snappers from the dailies were crowded round you.

"I think I've come to the end of the film," says Mam as her winder-onner meets resistance.

"Take it anyway!"...

Standard issue: Andy Starmore, ready for action back in the day.

THE UTILITY MAN

One hundred and fifty years ago in a Northern mill town, in the midst of the Industrial Revolution, top-hatted industrialists boasting names like Scriventhorpe, Blatherwycke and Blenkinsop first discovered a new way to squeeze an extra ounce of productivity out of their workforce. The division of labour saw the end of an enjoyable day's work doing all the various tasks

Unfortunately, neither did the early football industry escape the attentions of the middle-class organisers and managers – and it's still hampered by their influence.

Children aren't allowed to chase the ball, to goalhang and score. Oh, no.

Across all football history, it's taken an exceptional individual to break the mould and roam about the pitch in as

took an exceptional player to roam about the pitch adopting as many made-up positions as Ron Jeremy.

necessary to knit a jumper – sheeping, degaggling, plumping, purling – and the start of a tedious new regime of specialisation which involved pushing a loom backwards and forwards 43,000 times per day.

Right up until that fateful day in 2013 when the last industrial job in Britain was exported to China, production lines were similarly blighted by the squalid, tedious logic of the time-and-motion man.

many real and made-up positions as Ron Jeremy – the great John Charles for one.

We wouldn't want our teams playing total football, like the Dutch side of the 1970s, would we? And as for Paul Madeley, the Leeds stalwart who started the game in every number shirt from 2 to 11 during his career, we'll never see his like again.

Now go and stand in the far left-hand corner of the pitch, and do as you're told.

The groundbreaking, bright, sexy and dare we say it groovy United threads supplied by Admiral between 1973 and 1981.

ADMIRAL

Hands up who reckons the best Leeds United kits in history were the groundbreaking, bright, sexy and dare we say it groovy threads supplied by Admiral between 1973 and 1981.

In the 1970s, the first manufacturers' logos were beginning to appear on football shirts, and it was the Leicester-based Admiral company who seized on the possibilities of commercialising strips. Bert Patrick, chairman of Cook & Hurst, had formed an idea born out of England's 1966 World Cup win and the advent of colour TV. If kits could be uniquely designed and visibly branded then contracts with clubs could be signed, and the parents of young football fans would have to buy Admiral kit rather than the plain, generic shirts currently available.

Don Revie's fondness for making a bit of brass to supplement his salary at Leeds was a big help in the early days. Leeds were the first to wear the nautical trademark. Then, when Revie became England boss, a £16,000 deal was cut and

England's traditional plain white shirt was suddenly adorned with red-and-blue sleeve stripes and a yellow logo, much to the horror of traditionalists and to the delight of schoolboys across the nation. That shirt was the must-have item of 1975, and when Manchester United were also signed up, Admiral had the 'Big Three'. The rest quickly fell into line.

In every copy of *Shoot!* there would be a full-page colour advert showing their latest designs; there was an Admiral Annual which showed only photos of games in which both sides wore the approved brand; and you could send off for a poster which displayed every Admiral kit from Orient to Aberdeen.

Inevitably, bigger boys Adidas, Umbro and Le Coq Sportif caught up with, and overtook, the pioneering Admiral; but for a few glorious years at the end of the Seventies, Admiral was boss.

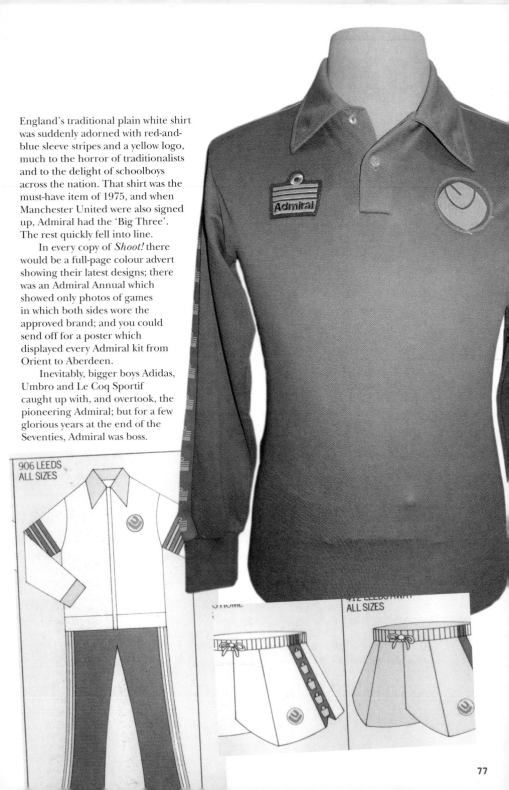

906 LEEDS
ALL SIZES

ALL SIZES

MUD

Mud used to be as central to the game of football as the ball itself. Placed on a freshly repainted centre-spot. By the Man in the Middle.

Mud was synonymous with football, a crucial factor in its tactics, skills and disciplines. We played in mud and paid to watch better players struggle to overcome mud – their control, balance and ability to dive and tackle like demons all dependent on mud.

Sometimes, even games as prestigious as the FA Cup Final were played on mud. In 1970 the final was played a month earlier than usual to allow England to acclimatise for the

Mexico World Cup. Leeds and Chelsea had to make do with a surface that had been churned up by the 'Horse of the Year Show' just a week previously.

From the terraces, football smelled of mud. On big occasions, we sneaked on to the pitch and helped ourselves to hallowed clumps of mud.

Best of all, on Saturday morning, we picked the dried, inverted mudprint out of our studs – a perfect, stud-holed fossil record of last weekend's 6-0 defeat – tossed it on the changing-room floor and started all over again, temporarily clean and full of hope for what the mud might bring.

Bring back 1970?
When the Cup Final was played in a
Horse of the Year Show mudbath...

LEAGUE DIVISION ONE
LEEDS UNITED v EVERTON
SAT · 1 JAN · 1977

Official Match Day

LEEDS UNITED

OFFICIAL MATCH DAY PROGRAMME PRICE 20p No. 14

FOOTBALL LEAGUE DIVISION ONE   MONDAY 1st JANUARY, 1979

NOTTINGHAM FOREST

In This Issue . . .

Jimmy Adamson's New Year message.

Tony Currie looks forward to 1979

Some of the Christmas presents United should have received plus a welcome to the League Champions, a United - France...

OFFICIAL MATCHDAY PROGRAMME No. 22
PRICE 35p

Wednesday 4th December 1974... Division One... K.O. 7.30
price 12p

PROGRAMMED TO EXPLODE

Leeds United v Tottenham 4th December 1974... KO 7.30 ... 12 pence.

    Jimmy Armfield Talking... "Those in absolute favour of freedom of contract would say that, with the end of payment of transfer fees, the game would easily be able to afford the possible consequences. But would it really? Our existing system is watertight. A player knows that unless he asks for a transfer he is bound to a club usually for something like four years. Consequently he is not subjected to approaches from other clubs which can only unsettle him."

LEEDS UNITED

LEAGUE DIVISION...
25th November...
MANCHESTER CITY

OFFICIAL MATCHDAY PROGRAMME PRICE 50p

TONIGHT'S MATCH SPONSORS
CIS INSURANCE
and
danepak

LEEDS UNITED

FA CHALLENGE CUP THIRD ROUND

Friday 4th January 1985

EVERTON

BARCLAYS LEAGUE DIVISION TWO
LEICESTER CITY
Saturday 28th April 1990

Official Matchday Magazine £1

F.A. CUP 5th ROUND
SATURDAY FEBRUARY 21st 1987
KICK OFF 3.00 P.M.

QUEENS PARK RANGERS

TODAY'S MATCH SPONSORS
DUNLOP & RANKEN STEEL SERVICES

No 08350

Official
Programme 5p

LEEDS

versus AST

Wednesday, 11th October, 1972

PETER LORIMER, ALLAN CLARKE and

Leeds United

WHITE SHIRTS, WHITE SHORTS
Colours:
1. DAVID HARVEY
2. PAUL MADELEY
3. TREVOR CHERRY
4. BILLY BREMNER
5. JACK CHARLTON
6. NORMAN HUNTER
7. PETER LORIMER
8. ALLAN CLARKE
9. MICK JONES
10. MICK BATES
11. TERRY YORATH
Sub.

Referee : Mr P. PARTRIDGE, Midd
Linesmen : Mr G. M. TREVETT, Man
Mr R. CHADWICK, Darw

Norman Hunter Testimonial Year: Don't miss the glittering Sportsman's Quiz at the Clock Cinema, Harehills on December 19th. International stars Terry Cooper, Johnny Giles, Gordon McQueen and Norman himself, stage a special play entitled Illegal Approach during the course of the evening.

I'm in Charge: Clive Thomas of Treorchy, who officiated in the Poland v Argentina and Brazil v East Germany World Cup games during the summer, was on Norwich City's books.

Wineways, Stainbeck Road – Where the best costs less. VAT 69 Whisky, £2.48; Dubonnet Red, £1.08; Double Century Sherry, £1.09.

Terry Neill Spurs Boss: "No Spectator after spending five hard days at work wants to come along to a football ground and merely see 22 workmen out there – he wants to be entertained."

The Facts: After 19 games, Leeds are 13th in the First Division. Top scorer is Allan Clarke with 8, and attendances are averaging 33,147.

Travel Away: To West Ham.. M1 south, A1, North Circular, turn right at East Ham.

Sports and Souvenir Shop: "Tie a Skelp around your wrist, wrap them around your neck or head, or tie one around your waist." 45p inc. p&p.

Hofbrauhaus, Merrion Centre: Fully Licensed, Bavarian and English foods, live entertainment nightly...

AL MATCHDAY PROGRAMME · PRICE 50p

TODAY'S MATCH SPONSOR
DUNLOP
RANKEN

LEEDS
UNITED

CANON LEAGUE DIVISION TWO

Saturday 30th November 1985

NORWICH CITY

Lion
Carpets

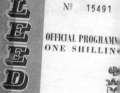

LEEDS
UNITED

No 15491

OFFICIAL PROGRAM
ONE SHILLIN

Derby
WEDNESDAY, 7th FEBR

NEXT H
SATURDAY, 10th FEBRU
West H
SATURDAY, 17th FEBR
NOTTING

LEEDS
UNITED
FOOTBALL

are you
IF NOT
enquiries
The Pools

SCARF ACE

The 1970s brought us so many new technological miracles, most of which had been unthinkable before the advent of the Space Race, the pressurised inventiveness of NASA and the resulting seven-iron shot on the moon. There was the digital watch with the numbers that glowed red; that tennis video game that went beep boop; video recorders and non-stick saucepans and portable calculators... and most astonishing of all, the unprecedented ability to print photographs onto fabric.

At first we had Six Million Dollar Man pyjamas
and Osmonds T-shirts...

At first we had Six Million Dollar Man pyjamas and Osmonds T-shirts. Then Major Sports Ltd transferred the hot new technology to the football scarf market and 'picture scarves' were suddenly available for all the top club and Home International sides, up to and including Wales.

Who needed the Bionic Woman, the Bay City Rollers or the Wombles when you could have Brian Flynn and Terry Yorath portrayed in glorious polyester pixels?

SHIRT SWAPPING

Have you any idea how much confusion Leeds caused the neutral fan of a certain innocent age by winning the Fairs Cup in 1971?

There was just no way to figure out how Leeds had played in their usual all-white but then appeared to be lifting the trophy in blue shirts with a yellow star.

Had they actually lost but the caption was wrong?

Even to more mature fans, it just looked all wrong. But at least they had the advantage of being aware of the ritual of shirt-swapping, which enabled them to work out that they were Juventus away shirts.

Leeds had played in white but lifted the trophy wearing blue...

Had they actually lost, and the caption was wrong?

UMBRO

Umbro have been making fantastic football kits since 1924, when the HUMphreys BROthers Harold and Wallace set up a workshop in Wilmslow, Cheshire. In those less ostentatious days, labels were worn on the inside of clothes rather than the outside, so their prestigious list of classic kits remained largely anonymous.

Blackpool's famous FA Cup triumph of 1953, Tottenham's 1961 Double, England's World Cup glory in 1966, Celtic's European Cup win in Lisbon in '67 and Manchester United's the following year were all achieved in Umbro kit, with not a visible diamond in sight.

The Umbro diamond
got its big-match debut
on Leeds' shirts at the
1973 Cup Final.

The little diamond logo started to appear on football shirts around 1973, Leeds and Sunderland both displaying them in the 1973 FA Cup Final. Then Everton, Burnley, Sheffield United and Birmingham... until, on the eve of the 1976-77 season, an advert appeared in *Shoot!* proclaiming: "It's going to be a sparkling season... just look at those diamonds!"

Leeds United
Home   Away   Track suit

Six years after Brazil had won the 1970 World Cup in Umbro without a single diamond showing, the new range of Umbro kits now sported dozens, with multi-logoed tape down the sleeves and shorts.

However, Leeds had abandoned Umbro halfway through the 1973-74 title-winning season.

Umbro returned to Elland Road for the 1981-82 season with a smart alternate yellow and blue pin-striped shirt that lasted for three season.

Four more decent designs followed through the '80s and into the '90s as Leeds emerged from the Second Division wilderness to get promoted under Howard Wilkinson, and then relive the glory days by bagging the last old-style League Championship before the Premier League steamroller arrived.

In the cutting-edge fashion race that football kits became, Umbro tried out all sorts of ideas: pin-stripes; shadow stripes; button-down collars; an Edwardian revival with lace-up collars; reversible shirts; a horrible grey England change strip that 'looked good with jeans'; and a refined 'tailored' plain white England shirt that went down very well... though in our opinion they never topped that first range.

Sadly, having been swallowed up and spat out by American giants Nike, Umbro's future looks to be in some doubt.

It's probably just as well that Harold Humphreys – described as 'the Dior of the football world' by the Daily Express in 1963 – isn't still around to witness England's new Nike kit.

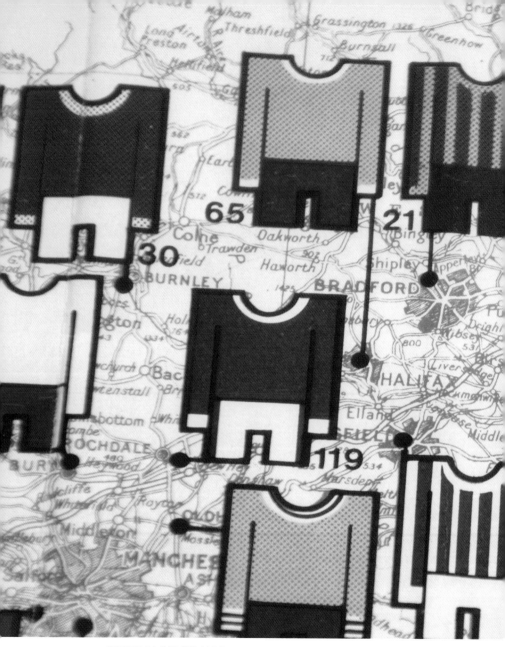

BARTHOLOMEW MAP

In the early 1970s John Bartholomew & Son produced the 'Football History Map of England and Wales' as part of their series of pictorial and historical maps…

Created by John Carvosso, the stylised square kits and re-rendered club crests gave it an iconic look that remains hugely popular among football supporters. In the years just before more intricate kit designs arrived this was all that was required.

It was a best seller among maps which gave a generation of football fans a solid foundation in geography… well, we knew where the towns with football clubs were, at least.

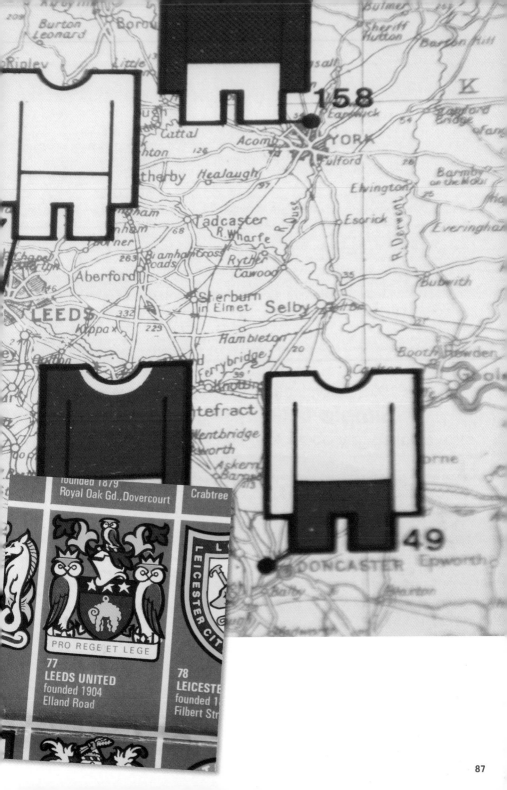

158

49

LEEDS BEATS

What's the finest Leeds-related choon ever captured on record?

Strictly in terms of the Leeds count, the 1972 FA Cup Final single 'Leeds United' (aka 'Glory, Glory, Leeds United') loses out to its own b-side, 'Leeds! Leeds! Leeds!' (aka 'Marching On Together') but there's no doubt that they've got it covered between them, and that the all-time number one is one of these Elland Road standards. They were both recorded with Don Revie's boys on vocals, who then strode up to number 10 in the UK singles chart at the end of the season.

Or how about 'Strings for Yasmin' by Tin Tin Out, which was played before kick-off for years – like 'Marching On Together' – but only up until the 2008-09 season?

Then there's Jack Charlton's solo 45 from 1972, the hilariously maudlin Chrimbo talkover, 'Simple Little Things', which was allegedly about the Man U forward line. Well worth looking up on YouTube for a laugh.

A couple of years earlier, Charlton, Terry Cooper and Norman Hunter were at the top of the charts on England's 'Back Home' 45 in 1970. Right from the big cha-cha cha-cha-cha intro, the horn-driven romp epitomises everything a World Cup song should be. Jeff Astle's finest moment leading the

Big Jack's 1972 solo single,
'Simple Little Things',
was allegedly about the Man U forward line.

All together now:
"Glory, glory,
Leeds United..."

line for England stirs and bonds: while we're watching the lads on the box, they're thinking about us, the folks back home. Forget your arsey postmodern irony: jut your chin and fight back the tears.

The weird circular triple-gatefold package of the 'World Beaters Sing The World Beaters' LP includes more era-defining tracks including 'Ob-La-Di, Ob-La-Da' with Norman and Terry on backing vocals, and 'There'll Always Be An England', featuring Big Jack.

Unfortunately, the 1974 World Cup follow-up by the England World Cup Squad (including Paul Madeley, Norman Hunter, Allan Clarke and future White Tony Currie) was less successful, having been recorded before they were knocked out in the qualifiers by Poland.

"England's having a ball / What a day for one and all": that was the imagined outcome of England's first World Cup qualification campaign since 1962; but even without the intervention of Poland and Peter Shilton, this fixed-grimace perkiness would never have made the charts. Even now, the misplaced optimism still has the power to wound.

Meanwhile, the Scotland World Cup Squad's effort was 'Easy Easy', a Bay City Rollers cast-off notable only for the rhyming of "Yaba-daba-doo" with "We are the boys in blue."

THE SMILEY ERA

In order to mould an all-new 'Super Leeds' image, the cash-conscious Don Revie hired local entrepreneur-artist-PR guru Paul Trevillion (former *Roy of the Rovers* cartoonist and early football agent!) to help maximise turnover from the fans. And *The Beaver* soon magicked up a complete beauty makeover, with maximum gimmickry.

Now the Leeds players would warm up with synchronised callisthenics and skilful set pieces on the field, wearing snazzy tracksuits with their names on the back. Before kick-off, they stood in a line and waved.

Strangely, the authorities mistook the intimidating stunts for the way forward, doubtless dreaming of a

distant, family-friendly cash bonanza –
and now, of course, every modern team
lines and waves to earn their corn.

Trevillion also made two iconic
contributions to Seventies football lore:
irresistible, pocket money-priced sock-
tags, designed to be autographed and
thrown into the crowd after the match,
and the classic 'LU' Smiley badge –
another ironic masterpiece.

Leeds _____ v _____ Coventry

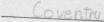

COLOUR ME BAD

Back in the day, I spent many hours scribbling away at the coarse paper of Caversham's *Football Colouring Book*, tongue lolling out to one side in sheer concentration, transforming the black outlines into lifelike and vibrant living colour. As you can see, I hardly ever went over the lines and had an almost eerie command of every stroke.

Leeds' vanilla ice-cream (the easiest one of all), Manchester United's crimson, West Ham's puce and blue, Hull's glowing amber and Liverpool's scarlet (achieved by pressing a bit harder than the crimson) were all portrayed to perfection under my artistic spell, now brought to life before your very eyes in a spectral rhapsody.

Just one tiny problem to prick my dreamlike bubble: "WHO'S GOT FELT PEN ON THE CARPET?!"

SUN SOCCERSTAMPS

Long before the hilarious horrors of
Sun Soccercards emerged at the end
of the Seventies, *The Sun* newspaper
bunged out a set of well-designed and
sensitively considered collectables on an
unexpected philatelic theme.

What we're trying to say is... they were
stamps.

Sun Soccerstamps, to be precise. The equal
best thing to happen in 1971, along with those
Esso badges; but definitely more highbrow!

Sun readers were invited to send in six
tokens and a 5p bit (Sellotaped to cardboard,
natch) in exchange for 12 Soccerstamps. And
you could use them on letters, too. Allegedly.

Billy Bremner

FIRST DIVISION CLUBS

LEEDS UNITED

Club Address: Elland Road, Leeds LS11 0ES
Telephone: Leeds 76037
Colours: All white strip
Founded: 1920
Nickname: 'The Peacocks'

Winners of the European Fairs Cup last season
was some consolation for Leeds United, but
the big prize of the League Championship was
snatched out of their hands by Arsenal. This
followed the heartbreak of the previous season
when they finished runners-up to Everton, Cup
runners-up to Chelsea and semi-finalists in the
European Cup.

After Leeds City had been wound up by the
F.A. in 1919 following an investigation into
illegal payments to players. United were formed
in 1920 and admitted into Division Two.
Full list of honours: Division One champions
1968-69,   runners-up 1964-65,   1965-66,
1968-70 and 1970-71. Division Two champions
1923-24,   1963-64.   runners-up 1927-28.
1931-32. 1955-56. F.A. Cup runners-up in
1965 and 1970. League Cup winners 1968.
Fairs Cup winners 196?   ?? and 1970-71 and
beaten finalists in 1966?
Famous players incl??   ??, Willis
Edwards, Bert Spr??   Con
Martin, John Cha??

Captain

Club Crest

1971-72 Team

Space for
Soccerstamp
No. 9

The token for the
colour soccerstamp
to go in this space
appears in The *Sun*

1st DIVISION TEAMS

GREAT GOALIES

GARY SPRAKE

YOUR ??????ATE SOCCERSTAMPS

If you ar? ?een Soccerstamp collector, you'll
almost certainly accumulate a number of
duplicates. But you can put these duplicate
Soccerstamps to good use because someone near
you – a friend, neighbour, classmate or workmate –
probably wants the very stamps you don't.
Throughout England there are over half a million
Soccerstamp collectors, so it shouldn't be too
difficult to contact one with whom to exchange
duplicates. And remember that you can always
form a Soccerstamp club at your factory, school,
office or local. Watch THE SUN for full details and
application forms.

THE Sun

REMEMBER THAT SOCCERSTAMP TOKENS APPEAR
EVERY DAY, MONDAY TO SATURDAY, IN THE SUN

95

gham City
ded 1875.
. 1921, 48, 55.
up 1963.
al blue

Blackburn Rovers
Founded 1874.
Div 1 1912, 14.
Div 2 1939. FA Cup 1884.
85, 86, 90, 91, 1928.
Blue & white

Blackpool
Founded 1887.
Div 2 1930.
Div I runners-up 1956.
FA Cup 1953.
Tangerine & white

Bolton Wanderers
Founded 1874.
Div 2 1909.
FA Cup 1923, 26, 29, 58.
All white

Bradford City
Founded 1903.
Div 2 1908.
Div 3 (N) 1929.
FA Cup 1911.
Claret & amber

Brighton & Hove Albion
Founded 1900.
Div 3 (S) 1958.
Div 4 1965.
Blue & white

Bristol City
Founded 1894.
Div 2 1906.
Div 3 (S) 1923, 27, 55.
All red

Bristol Rovers
Founded 1883.
Div 3 (S) 1953.
Sky blue & white
Di

verton
1878. Div 1 1891.
. 32, 39, 63, 70.
v 2 1931.
p 1906, 33, 66.
ue & white

Falkirk
Founded 1876.
Sc Div 2 1936, 70.
Sc Cup 1913, 57.
Navy blue & white

Football Club Badges

The Esso collection of 76 famous football club badges.
When you've completed this card you'll have a permanent record of the most famous
football clubs in England, Northern Ireland, Scotland and Wales represented
by their unique and colourful insignias. Keep it safe – you will own what may become
a valuable collector's item.

EC European Cup. ECWC European Cup Winners' Cup. EFC European Fairs Cup. FL Football League. Sc Scottish. SLC Scottish League Cup.

anchester City
d 1894. Div 1 1937.
v 2 1899, 1903, 10.
. 66. FA Cup 1904.
. 69. FL Cup 1970.
1970. Blue & white

Manchester United
Founded 1878. Div 1 1908,
11, 52, 56, 57, 65, 67.
Div 2 1936. FA Cup 1909.
48, 63. EC 1968.
Red & white

Swansea City
Founded 1911.

D UNITED
F C
1889

Sheffield United
Founded 1889.
Div 1 1898.
Div 2 1953.
up 1899, 1902, 15, 25.
Red, white & black

Sheffield Wednesday
Founded 1867. Div 1 1903,
04, 29, 30. Div 2 1900,
26, 52, 56, 59.
FA Cup 1896, 1907, 35.
Blue & white

Shrewsbury Town
Founded 1886.
Elected to League 1950.
Welsh Cup twice.
All blue

Southampton
Founded 1885.
Div 3 (S) 1922.
Div 3 1960.
Red, white & black

ESSO CLUB BADGES

What was your favourite set of freebies
given away with petrol back in the day?
Nowadays, it's hard to imagine anything
but a form for a mortgage being
handed out by the garage man, as it
costs the same now to fill your tank as it
did to buy your first car. But this hasn't
always been the case.

While the likes of Texaco and Shell
seemed obsessed with making huge
amounts of money by flogging us the
world's overflowing natural resources,
back in 1971 good old Esso were only

Leeds United
Founded 1920.
Div 1 1969.
Div 2 1924, 64.
FL Cup 1968. EFC 1968.

WEMBLEY METTOY BILLY

Most of the experiences and objects within these covers relate to things that we knew first-hand or were at least aware of back in the day. But this Wembley Mettoy figure... never owned one, never even heard of them until recently. And yet it still manages to stir a certain something within my ten-year-old self which lurks just under the surface of my skin. I loved models, I loved football, I would *really* have loved one of these.

The English language doesn't seem to have a word for feelings of nostalgia for something you never knew. The Germans have *sehnsucht* (thoughts about facets of life that are unfinished or imperfect, paired with a yearning for ideal alternative experiences), while Portuguese has *saudade* (related to thinking back on situations of privation due to the absence of someone or something).

Somewhere in an alternative universe, this little Billy would have been taken down from my shelf every week for a carpet-level kickaround with Charlie George, George Best, Martin Chivers and Bobby Moore – probably in slow-motion, with breathy crowd noise effects.

I would get one from eBay, as a sort of nostalgia experiment, but a Mettoy Bremner with no box or name label is going for £26.99... *saudade*, indeed.

concerned with making sure that small boys had plenty of great football stuff to collect. First, there were World Cup coins, then 'Squelchers', a series of little booklets so named because the info contained in them was enough to squelch any argument. There were FA Cup Winners coins, and the Top Team Collection of Photo-Discs built a squad of Britain's best players... but one of the best was surely the literally titled 'Esso Collection of Football Club Badges'.

Esso even provided a splendid fold-out presentation card to stick them in and, frankly, if there was anything more exciting happening in 1971, we can't remember it now. It wasn't just the 20p blackmail job for the 'Starter Pack' of 26 otherwise unobtainable badges that made the heart beat faster. The little foil badges were irresistible. Everyone was collecting them.

Have you still got yours?

WEMBLEY

"Based on the English Football Association Challenge Cup Competition, the most gripping features and exciting uncertainties of which it reproduces with vivid and truly amazing fidelity..."

No one plays board games any more: it's all down to attention span and lack of imagination and wanting excitement served up on a plate instead of having to work at it. And that's just us, never mind the kids.

It was the thrill of the Cup draw and the possibility of an alternative-universe upset that used to make Wembley so addictive. The reproduction of all those associations and assumptions that electrify the simple twinning of two clubs' names ("And it's Leeds United... at home to... "Huddersfield Town"... or "Manchester United"... or "Bradford City"... we could go on).

It was the tension inherent in the inevitable reduction of 32 clubs to an historic final pairing. The chance to witness a spunky lower-league outfit confound the Darwinian bias that enabled top clubs to make more money, to spend it on star players, to score more goals... and even claim the right to throw loaded dice.

"The earning ability of clubs varies greatly, as does their playing ability," stated the Rules of the Game. "Each club has a value (representing gate receipts) and each Division has different colour dice for Home and Away matches. These dice are specially produced to give a built-in advantage both to teams in higher divisions and to teams playing at Home."

The powerful red First Division Home die could roll 0, 1, 2, 3 or two chances of a 4, while the white Third/Fourth Division Away die was lumbered with two 0s and two 1s – plus a potentially giant-killing 4 and a 5 to spice things up.

Bring on Colchester!

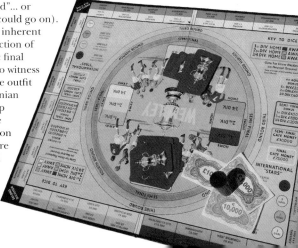

THE WRONG TROUSERS

Oh, the shame of it – those odd occasions in the past when the kit-man takes his eye off the ball and your team have to rummage around in the lost-property box like the kid who left his PE kit at home.

It seems that goalkeepers were especially prone to wrongkititis: here's Leeds United and Scotland's David Harvey mixing club with country, and Umbro with Admiral.

One of our favourite wardrobe malfunctions is the upside-down Leeds 'Smiley' badge as it appeared on the cover of the *Football League Review*.

When the badge was first introduced, someone, somewhere had the job of sewing them on to the shirts, and hadn't realised that they were supposed to read 'LU'...

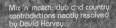

Mix 'n' match: club and country contradictions neatly resolved by David Harvey.

97

"W.A.C.C.O.E!"

MATCH WEEKLY

Match Weekly was launched on 6 September 1979, three weeks into the 1979-80 season, by Peterborough-based publishers EMAP. Editor Melvyn Bagnall declared: "Our object is simple... to improve on anything currently available." By which, of course, he meant *Shoot!*, which had enjoyed a relatively unopposed decade of market dominance.

What immediately grabbed this 13-year-old about the newcomer on the newsagent's shelf was the way it was printed right to the edge, making *Shoot!*'s white borders suddenly look very passé.

Inside there was a stellar line-up of writers: Keegan, Clough, Ardiles, Coppell, Atkinson and Jimmy Hill. Instead of 'Focus On' there was 'Match Makers', with loads more questions. There were more colour pages, and 'Match Facts' with marks out of ten for

Inside this week:
Leeds United teamgroup!

every player in every game. And, just in case anyone was still dithering about parting with their 25p, there was a free Transimage sticker album thrown into the mix.

After a five-year love affair with *Shoot!*, I jumped ship to *Match* in an instant. And I wasn't the only one. After a long battle, *Match* eventually won out with a higher circulation.

CHARITY SHIELD

Since 1908 the Charity Shield had been treated like a mixed metaphor of dog's dinner and moveable feast. Touring all the big grounds from Highbury to Goodison, it eventually settled on a formula of League Champions vs. FA Cup Winners. However, by the early Seventies, its stock was pretty low.

In 1973 it should have been contested by Sunderland and Liverpool, but neither could be bothered, so holders Manchester City played Second Division champions Burnley at Maine Road.

When neither Liverpool nor Leeds showed much enthusiasm in fulfilling the fixture the following year, the FA decided to elevate its kudos by staging it at Wembley. They probably soon wished they hadn't, as a dirty game descended into fisticuffs with Billy Bremner and Kevin Keegan becoming the joint first British players to be dismissed under

It wasn't an ideal season opener for the FA,
but, for the rest of us, it was fantastic stuff.

We're off!
Micro Billy and
micro Kev stomp
off under imaginary
Twin Towers.

the Twin Towers, both throwing off their shirts on the way to the tunnel. As far as the FA were concerned, this was neither charitable nor the ideal curtain-raiser to the new season, and both players were handed eleven-game suspensions. For the rest of us, it was fantastic stuff, the only one we can remember, and certainly the only Charity Shield ever to feature in a film...

BAG TAG

During our time at secondary school we invented a game that was so good we were convinced it would be adopted by every twelve-year-old boy in the land, sweeping across Britain like a forest fire; but somehow it didn't.

All you needed to make dinner-hour a time of high-octane excitement was a tennis ball. The rest of the equipment you already lugged round with you all day. Your bag.

Whether the cheapo variety with 'Sports' printed on the side; or a pricier Adidas' bag (with 'all day I dream about sex' added in felt pen) we placed them in a circle, the size of which was determined by the number of players. The rules were simple, as indeed were we. You could only touch the ball with your feet. Your bag was your own individual goal. If the ball hit your bag you had one life left – a second hit and you were out of the game. You had to strike a balance between defending your own bag and forming alliances to attack someone else's. There was plenty of scope for subterfuge and double bluff and just as in *Macbeth* (which we would be studying later that day in English), overreaching ambition could swiftly lead to your downfall.

All you need is an Adidas bag
(with 'all day I dream about sex' added in felt pen).

Location, location, location:
Through the tunnel to the training pitch,
a hot spot in *The Damned United* film.

ACTION TRANSFERS

It isn't every club who got their own Letraset set, but Leeds got lucky around the time of the 1972 Cup Final against Arsenal. Even so, the full glory of the Action Transfer isn't captured until you see them artistically applied to a scene...

This is easy. All you have to do is scribble the transfers off their greaseproof-paper backing on to the empty pitch in front of the Kop, and soon you'll have an action-packed Instant Picture™ of a match as good as anything a photographer could produce.

Now then. Let's 'peel away backing paper' and kick off with one of the White-and-Violet team realistically booting the ball upfield. While his goalie jumps around out of his area. And one of the

Turquoises throws a dummy on the edge of the box. While another one goes for a diving header sitting on his team-mate's shoulders.

It's no use the Letraset bods flagging up the deadly danger of failing to 'slide backing paper under other pictures to avoid accidental transfer' – it's already too late for the centre-forward's head. What we really need is more players just hanging around, like in real life, gossing and blowing on their hands and doing leg stretches...

Paramount Picture Corporation, 1970. Printed by Letraset Ltd., Patented.

GK 122/16   Patented. Printed in England by Letraset Ltd.

...one using some of your instant pictures.

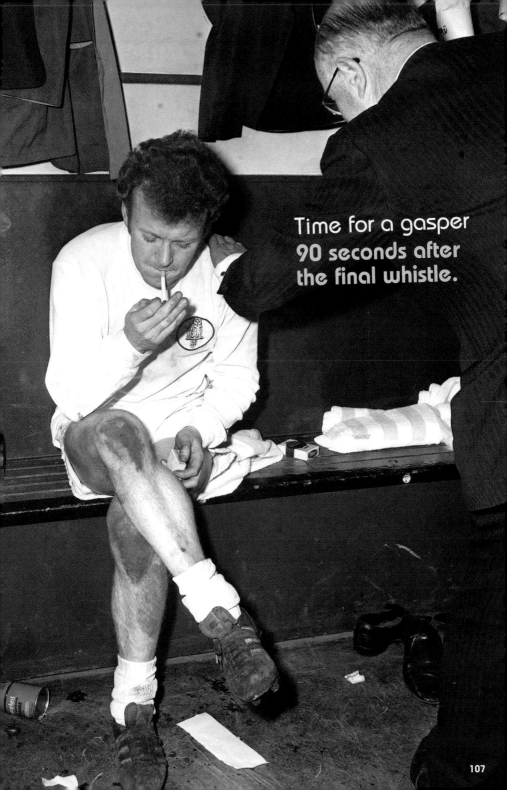

Time for a gasper
90 seconds after
the final whistle.

So how to let it be known which side you were supporting in the big Cup game on Saturday? That's where white rosettes with yellow and blue trim came in: they were the acceptable face of partisanship in more restrained times.

You don't get them any more.

THE ROSETTE

In the olden days, British males over the age of six were only permitted to wear brown, grey, greeny-brown, browny-green or, in moments of extreme flamboyance, navy.

If a chap had worn a football jersey anywhere other than on a football field he might well have been assumed to be quite insane, and arrested for causing a breach of the peace. And the same applied to sporting any item of apparel other than a school blazer in a primary colour. Red socks and yellow waistcoats, for example, were only ever sported by show-offs, buffoons and variety acts.

SUN SOCCERCARDS

Allow us to whisk you back to
the tail end of the '70s, and
one particular night beloved of
many football card collectors.
The night in question was
notable for the long, gruelling,
coffee-fuelled marathon
undertaken by the anonymous
Sun Soccercard artist, chained
to his desk with a dozen packs of
big bright felt pens and ordered to

It took a long, gruelling, coffee-fuelled marathon
to produce this Arthur Graham.

produce a set of nearly 1,000 player
likenesses (or as near as possible
in the case of poor old Arthur
Graham).

The results speak for themselves.
But just in case you don't recognise
your heroes of yesteryear, here's...
well, let's just hope their old mums
don't recognise them either!

Anything to avoid paying image
rights, eh? Even if the man with the
felt-pen never did quite
get the hang of eyes, their
size relative to the human
head, and the fact that
they're usually pretty
much on the same
level.

SUN SOCCERCARD No 68 — F. GRAY (Scotland)

SUN SOCCERCARD No 823 — R. HANKIN (Leeds United)

SOCCERCARD No 512 — B. STEVENSON (Leeds United)

SUN SOCCERCARD No 65 — A. GRAHAM (Scotland)

SUN SOCCERCARD No 43 — T. CURRIE (England)

SUN SOCCERCARD No 58 — B. FLYNN (Wales)

SUN SOCC...ARD No 218 — B. BREMNER (Scotland)

You're not looking
yourself today:
Whites off colour
circa 1979.

SUN SOCCERCARD No 35 — T. COOPER (England)

SUN SOCCERCARD No 122 — P. MADELEY (England)

SUN SOCCERCARD No 109 — P. LORIMER (Scotland)

Leeds in red?
Yep, sometimes it was red shorts,
other times all red!?!

FOCUS ON...

Back in 1973, Leeds' Trevor John Cherry lay to shame every modern footballer who ever filled in a programme questionnaire namedropping property portfolios and £750 cocktails. Trev didn't like injuries, waiting or losing to Sunderland in the Cup Final, but he did like driving his Cortina GT, playing golf, roast beef 'n' Yorkshire pudding, Lulu and Greece.

And big (6ft 3ins) Jock Gordon McQueen tells it like it is. Or rather was. **FAVOURITE TV SHOW:** Benny Hill. **FAVOURITE SINGERS:** Yes, Moody Blues, Fairport Convention. **CAR:** Peugot 504.

Chicken in a basket, gym teacher, Raquel Welch and Benny Hill.

Gordon hated losing the European Cup-Winners' Cup Final to AC Milan, but at least he'd been to Holland. He was an honest soul: **IF YOU WEREN'T A FOOTBALLER WHAT DO YOU THINK YOU WOULD BE:** I dread to think. But just keep him away from his **BIGGEST DRAG IN SOCCER:** Injuries and bad refereeing. And feed him on his **FAVOURITE FOOD:** Chinese, anything made by Cadburys.

Michael John Giles, 5ft 6in, from Dublin, reveals his **FAVOURITE PLAYER:** Nobby Stiles, is also his brother-in-law, and his **MOST DIFFICULT OPPONENT:** Norman Hunter in practice games... but he keeps schtum on his **BIRTHDATE:** which is: "A secret!"

He likes golf, Morecambe & Wise, Johnny Mathis and Turkish singer Tung Ozbey.

His **PROFESSIONAL AMBITION:** is to win the European Cup... Ooooh, close but no cigar.

THE SCRAPPER

In the six million-year interval between man first walking upright and the invention of the 24-hour kids' TV channel, the PlayStation, the Xbox, the Wii and the DS, kids were faced with a bit of a challenge. How to fill all those long, boring hours before it was time to blow their candles out? It was merely hundreds of years ago when the penny finally dropped, and pastimes such as needlepoint, pressing wild flowers and making your own scrapbook at last began to gain popularity.

Most young football fans had a go at assembling scraps devoted to their football team, but few persisted for very long. The first page of every scrapbook is filled, the last page hardly ever. After a few weeks, cutting your club's match reports and photos out of the paper tended to become a chore, enabling you to later track the ever-decreasing degree of care with which they were Gloyed onto the coarse pages. And then there was that final time you jumped the gun and Dad found a comedy hole in the back of his *Sunday Express* before he'd finished with it...

between opponents with his eye on the ball, only occasionally glancing at the opponents' positions."

In other words, I booted the ball along and ran after it. Simple.

More troublesome was the accompanying lesson in the series: 'Running Without the Ball', a skill long unappreciated by the schoolboy masses. Running With and Without the Ball are like yin and yang. Halves of a whole. One muddy and exhausting; the other silent and all but unconscious, a product of Zenlike mind training.

LEARN THE GAME

For hours at a time, I would practise my skills out on the driveway, taking a break every couple of minutes to study the little diagrams on my Anglo Confectionery 'Learn The Game' football cards.

The only thing holding me back from performing the perfect scissor-kick was the slight disadvantage of never having seen Denis Law pulling off "the most spectacular of all kicks." So, I'd lob the ball up in the air, wait for it... then launch myself backwards, hanging upside-down in mid-air for graceful milliseconds before crumpling to the slabs.

Fittingly enough, it was Everton's Alan Ball who was used as the model pro to illustrate the more worldly skill of 'Running With the Ball'.

Following the letter of the law, I moved "at speed, rolling the ball with the outside, the inside, or the front of the instep." I observed "the feinting and body swerving" of the cartoon Ball, and mimicked the way he "finds his way

As the perfect counterbalance to Alan Ball, you might have expected Burnley's Peter No-Ball to pose for this one, but instead Leeds United's Mick Jones was nominated as the most accomplished... runner. Not necessarily the fastest, you understand: Running Without the Ball is all about anticipation and "moving cleverly into position."

I observed Jones "reading" the pattern of the game "and how intelligently he runs into an unmarked position where he expects his colleague will pass the ball."

I moved cleverly down the garden path as far as Ringo the Rabbit's run, then trotted intelligently back – anticipating that I'd be in for my tea before the Scissor-Kick or Running Without the Ball returned again to the top of the pack.

UP FOR THE CUPPA

In the season before the 1966 World Cup, those nice people at Ty-Phoo Tea were running a smashing offer whereby any thirsty fan could collect up packet tops and send off for a large 10" by 8" teamgroup card of their choice.

And sometimes you'd even get a little picture of a player printed on the side of the box, which kids would inevitably hack out with scissors almost before mum could get the tea (note, that's 'tea', not your common-as-muck not-yet-invented 'teabags') into the tea canister.

Nice cup of Rosie Lee with your eggy soldiers in the morning? And a nice little Gareth (Gary) Sprake on the side, with your triangular toast in a little metal stand to make it go cold extra quick...

One lump or two? The Norman Hunter mug conundrum.

115

Fans' eye view:
At the Charity Shield,
Wembley 1992.

THE SOUVENIR SHOP

There's a lot more going on down the ground than kicking a ball around these days. We're talking business-class banqueting, stadium tours, helicopter rides, a members-only gym, conference facilities and unlimited retail opportunities.

It's enough to make you yearn for the old-school souvenir shop, where they didn't sell corporate badged grooming sets (eyebrow notcher; beard sculptor; shower gel) or calendars of the playing staff printed last July, and

already way out of date. No black third kits, either. Every club has a black or grey third kit now because they 'look good with jeans' according to the PR man. Hey, all sizes other than XXL and XXXL are reduced to a mere 30 quid! Which is to say, 50 quid to you.

Bring back the rubbish old shop, where they only sold plastic caps, sew-on patches and programme binders. None of your new-fangled showy stuff like mugs, mind. And no need for bobble hats, because that's what grans were for.

100 PER CENT BEEF

"Th'maght loook the same but th'doon't taaste the same," reasoned the serious-faced little Yorkshire kid when his brother came up with a scheme that involved eating cheap beefburgers instead of Birds Eye, all so that t'Mam would then be able to save enough money to buy them groovy Leeds United tracksuits.

No chance. Even though Leeds were the biggest club in the country at the time this junior philosopher wasn't going to eat inferior burgers.

Cue voiceover as the advert ends: "Birds Eye Beefburgers – somehow, other beefburgers just don't taste the same."

coach to the match; a guided tour of the club's facilities; then reserved seats for the match with tea afterwards in the players' lounge..."

At LEEDS! The LEAGUE CHAMPIONS!

It seemed like a trip to Nirvana for any ten-year-old of the time. There were even 600 runners-up prizes of soccer watches, tracksuits and practice balls. You just couldn't lose.

Having successfully persuaded Mum of the merits of quality over economy in beef products, I carefully studied the Spot the Ball photo and agonised over where to place my fateful single cross.

I carefully cut out the packet

Fifty lucky winners would get to
"meet the Leeds team at their hotel for lunch..."

My problem was just the opposite. Persuading my mum to buy Birds Eye beefburgers instead of a cheap alternative, just so I could get hold of the 'Spot the Ball' form on the back of the packet, and go in for the most fantastic prize imaginable.

Fifty lucky winners of the first prize would "meet the Leeds team at their hotel for lunch; go on the players'

emblazoned with Billy Bremner, Joe Jordan, Peter Lorimer and the rest, and scraped together the coppers for a first-class stamp. I addressed my envelope to 408 Sydenham Road, Croydon CR0 2EA in my neatest handwriting, and ran to the post-box to ensure I beat the closing date of 31 August, 1974.

And then I waited.

I waited and waited and waited.

I waited on the bottom step in the hall and stared at the letter-box, willing a congratulatory letter to drop on the doormat.

"We are pleased to be able to tell you... please be at the Holiday Inn at... no need to bring any lunch, but an autograph book and a camera would be a good idea... please note that Leeds United AFC cannot be held responsible..." and so on. The fine print would be of more interest to Dad than me.

I waited for that letter. And waited. And waited.

I'm still waiting.

I'll settle for a practice ball.

BIRDS EYE

4 Beefburgers

Play "Spot the Ball" and join Leeds United

LEAGUE CHAMPIONS 73-74

FIRST DIVISION FOOTBALL INSIDE. LIVE THROUGH ATCH BUILD UP! SPEND A DAY WITH THE STARS OF TED, ALL EXPENSES PAID.

u have to do is "Spot the Ball" g new Birds Eye Beefburgers etition.

can win and take any grown se, even uncle Charlie. Grown nd bring any one of the kids n behaving themselves just

O FIRST PRIZES

cky winning pairs travel to t the team at their hotel for

unch the kids (that's those der 18) go in the players' natch. Grown ups travel

the kick-off everyone goes ur of the club's facilities. here'll be reserved seats for tea afterwards in the e.

nd of the day, each of the rts bag. Inside they'll find a their name on it, a football actice ball and an auto- of the team.

O RUNNERS UP

runners-up there are 200 pecial soccer watches, of track suits and 200 actice footballs. yone who enters has a fair ng.

PLUS MANY OTHER PRIZES

HOW TO PLAY

Study the photograph of the team in action and see if you can decide, using all your skill, the exact position the ball was in when we took the picture.

Then mark the spot with just one small cross in ink or ball point pen, fill in the coupon cut round the dotted line and send it together with the front of any Birds Eye Beefburger packet to the address below.

Birds Eye "Trip to Leeds" Competition, 408 Sydenham Road, Croydon, CRO 2EA.

Entry to the competition will be deemed to be acceptance of the competition rules. You will find them printed on the special "Spot the Ball" Beefburger packs at your local store. Or you can also get a copy by writing to the address above.

The competition closes 31st August 1974, so fill in your entry right away.

See you at the game.

NAME _____

ADDRESS _____

AGE _____

Parent/Guardian _____ (if under 18 Parents/Guardian's signature)

121

REMEMBER TO ENCLOSE YOUR PACK FRONT

Gotcha!
Gary 'Careless Hands' Sprake
kept over 200 clean sheets in 504 club appearances.

THE PARK DRIVE BOOK OF FOOTBALL

"In this book we pay tribute to many of the finest footballers in the country. It is not suggested in any way that mention of any individual implies that he is a smoker or in favour of any brand of cigarette." and shakers at the time, winning the League Cup in 1968 and the League title the following year. Don Revie wrote an article (without a hint of irony) titled "Is Modern Football Too Rough?"

Before players all started to have modern-day long hair, sideburns and V-neck collars.

Having cleared up any potential misunderstanding, we were left to plough into the 1968, 1969 and 1970 editions of the *Park Drive Book of Football*.

As I inherited all three at once, many years after they were first published – in 1973 – to me they were a wonderfully nostalgic read, before players all started to have modern-day long hair, sideburns and V-neck collars.

United were one of the big movers

"I wince when I watch the Leeds United players in training – they put as much effort into it as Olympic athletes. Afterwards they will sit in the dressing room picking each other to pieces and it is music to my ears! They constantly analyse each other's weaknesses, discussing ways to overcome them. And this shows they are striving for perfection all the time."

Whites make the cover! On no account ever break the spine of your own valuable vintage books.

MIND THE GAP

Pity the poor old modern pro, who must occasionally feel like a talented younger brother brought up by cantankerous parents in the shadow of a favourite elder son.

"Look at me, Dad. I've got football skills that weren't dreamed of back in the 1990s, and I've got a girlfriend who models fake all-over tan."

"Ah, you wouldn't have caught *Our Bobby* earning your kind of obscene money. I don't know, with your diamonds stuck all over your mobile phone and your little nicks cut out of your eyebrows."

"But Dad, I've been voted into the UK's Top 50 Eligible Celebrities by readers of *Eligible Celebrities* magazine."

"You know *Our Bobby* could down a gallon and then do a hundred press-ups on the bar? He was a proper head-turner was Our Bobby, especially when he put his teeth in..."

Fact is, today's pro can never compete with the players of even ten years ago precisely because he's so wealthy and talented, so polite and well turned out.

You wouldn't have caught Joe Jordan spending £50,000 on a pearl-white set of Gangsta gnashers. Joe had his four front teeth kicked out in a Leeds United reserve-team game: all the better to terrorise any unfortunate sod going up against him for a header, when he earned the horror-flick nickname of 'Jaws' without once resorting to cannibalism.

While on the way to Old Trafford from Elland Road during the 1978 World Cup, Joe was the star of a Heineken ad, where a pint of lager 'refreshed the parts other beers cannot reach'. Joe's teeth grew back,

temporarily, while fresh graffiti across the north of England claimed: 'Joe Jordan kicks the parts other beers cannot reach'.

Once he'd slipped out his false front teeth, Joe had nothing left to lose. Stripped for action, he stood outside any real-world concerns such as the desire to find a mate, or to eat an apple.

Compare and contrast with, ooh, let's say Ashley Cole...

UNFORGETTABLES

JOE JORDAN

GARY

JOE JORDAN

JOE JORDAN

JOE JORDAN

Heineken refreshes the parts other beers canno' reach.

125

KEEP FIGHTING

"Graham."
  "Present, sir."

"McQueen."
  "He's forgotten his kit, sir."

"Jordan?"
  "He's at the dentists's."

"Gemmill...?"

SCOTTISH SUPERSTARS

Up until twenty years ago, every great First Division team in football history had included at least one Scot, usually the brains of the operation – the ball player, the stopper who could do more than just stop, or the unstoppable goalscorer.

Leeds had Billy Bremner, arguably the most hated player in British football, but only by opposing teams and their fans – who would have given anything to see the wee wind-up merchant in their team's colours, especially alongside fellow Scot Peter Lorimer. Then there was McQueen and Jordan and Graham.

For the twelve years between the World Cups of 1970 and 1982, all of Britain took a special interest in the Scots as, time and time again, England failed to take the baby steps up on the world stage. With so many familiar, gifted players, they became everyone's second team. Well, who were we supposed to support? Iran?

The Scots heap derision on our temporary switching of allegiances thirty years ago. In the same position, they now wear 'Anyone But England' T-shirts, and we wouldn't want it any other way. But how sweet it would be to see Scotland return to dynasty-building form and make their first major championship this century; even back in the Home Internationals, so we can do our level best to beat their pasty bottoms.

Choose fitba.

If there were a World Cup for value, Avenger would win it.

The Chrysler Avenger.
Style, toughness. And a Championship performance.

CHRYSLER
UNITED KINGDOM

FLOODLIGHTS

Head tilted up to the heavens, the sight of a squally shower swirling through a floodlight beam was as close to God as many a football fan would ever get. Especially if the floodlight pylon (and the Supporters' Club bar) that had given rise to his epiphany were an after-thought addition to a crumbling barn of a terrace, home to an eternal denizen of the nether leagues.

The floodlight pylon was an object of awe, towering hundreds of feet over the crowd, hemming in the oblong mudbath with its three identical (or, better still, pathetically mismatched) brothers – naked iron-girder scaffolds tapering up into low cloud.

You have to look up to experience an intimation of the infinite, and your own insignificance. Hence church spires. City skyscrapers. Suicide pacts from suspension bridges. A row of 30 billion-Watt spotlights strung along the front of twin main stands just don't cut the mustard, let alone the long-banished fog.

And they were useful, too. How else was it possible to home in on an oppo ground on a 1970s Saturday motoring excursion? Seek the floodlights, and ye shall find.

Without the towering beacon of four majestic floodlight pylons

how are away fans supposed to find their way to the ground?

POCKET-MONEY ENDORSEMENTS

There's just one welcome side effect of every British professional footballer owning a private island off the coast near Bridlington, with a helicopter pad and a retractable Olympic-size swimming pool with a football pitch secreted underneath. Mercifully, football mags, programmes and comics are no longer cluttered up with embarrassing ads for cringeworthy products which the players have clearly never used in real life, but are still willing to put their name to in order to earn an extra 300 quid to throw away on the greyhounds.

Having said that, we're not so sniffy we wouldn't shove small children out of the way to get a go on Gordon Strachan's thrilling Centapost innovation, which he personally invented in his free time.

Disinterested observers from the United Nations have since backed up Gordon's claim that the apparently cumbersome yet oh-so-easily portable device, which lit up and made a bleeping noise when you kicked the ball against it, was indeed "the most exciting football invention since the ball." Which is why, even today, you rarely come across a park or a beach without a posse of young pros benchmarking their new-found skills on a futuristic digital scoreboard. Available any time now, yeah?

For some inexplicable reason, the stars of the great Leeds side of the 1960s and 1970s weren't in demand for endorsements as much as some of the more user-friendly football stars. That's why we loved the way Jackie Charlton elbowed in on Bobby Charlton's Casdon Soccer game blurb.

"Bobby Charlton says it is the nearest thing to English soccer it is possible to experience in one's own home," the box lid said, "and has spent many hours playing with his own family."

What a delicious thought, brother Jackie coming round to play with Bobby. No arguments about who would be white and who would be red.

Mover 'n' shaker: Nowadays, 99 per cent of all football goals have a left, a right and a centre post.

On the Kop:
Everything to play for...

CHANGING TO YELLOW

Nowadays, it appears that every football marketing man's erotic dream is an all-black second strip, perhaps with a sparing, luminous-green or pink trim. But there was a time when it was absolutely *costume de rigueur* to wear an all-yellow away kit – or 'amber' as the Umbro catalogue had it.

Leeds were probably the first, the yellow pioneers; but by the late Seventies it seemed that every club that had to change kits were trooping out of the tunnel

DUNCAN McKENZIE

like a bunch of bananas. These were more practical times and this wasn't done to sell shirts, but to avoid the need for a third kit as so few teams had yellow as a home strip.

Arsenal, Sunderland, Chelsea, Everton, Birmingham, Nottingham Forest, Charlton, Bristol Rovers,

PAUL MADELEY

Liverpool, Blackburn,
Tottenham and many
more – they were all
Leeds copycats, sporting
their own version of
mustard/sunflower/
canary/lemon/saffron
by the early Eighties, before
someone worked out that there might
be money to be made from more
frequent colour clashes...

TREVOR CHERRY

PAUL REANEY

Leeds were a **joyous ray of yellow sunshine** in the grim and brutal world of 70s football!

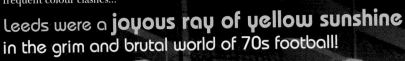

KEEPY-UPPY

The law of going up the reccie states: "Should there be six or more players available, they shall be divided into teams accordingly on a pitch size determined by the two captains. Should there be five, then they shall play cuppies – two teams of two kicking into one goal, taking turns as goalkeeper. And should there be three or under, they shall play keepy-uppy."

It takes two minutes to understand the rules of keepy-uppy and a lifetime to get past fifty.

The ball cannot touch the ground and should be constantly propelled upwards by feet, knees, thigh, chest or head.

One summer we did virtually nothing else and managed a glorious 72.

Here we see rare images from the grand Leeds United Keepy-Uppy Tournament of 1970. The rest of the team keep a critical eye on South African Albert Johanneson's juggling skills, Terry Cooper manages a well balanced 27; Johnny Giles a rather stiff 19; Terry Hibbitt an erratic nine.

Keep practising, lads…

CLUBCALL

Back in the Eighties and Nineties, it was the sheer unavailability of up-to-the-minute club information that made it so tantalising. So valuable.

You wouldn't want everyone else to know that Lee Chapman had a hammy, would you? – not if you were still thinking he might be playing Saturday. You wouldn't want to miss what 'Wantaway' Chris Whyte had allegedly denied this morning – or Wilko's counter-denials of any new ace African stoppers rumours. Ahh, the rumours…

LEEDS UNITED
CLUBCALL
— PHONE NOW —
0898 12 11 80

The Clubcall service came as a blessing for all fans – especially those exiled from local news and those trapped at work with the benefit of a free phone to avoid the disgraceful premium call rates.

At the end of the line – literally – was a local newspaper stringer (or at least an Ansafone recording of him) summing up back-page stories from yesterday's evening paper and this morning's tabs. To deliver value for money, he also used to make up juicy filler on the spot, and read it out. S-l-o-w-l-y.

"Hello… and it's a big… Whites… welcome… to your exclusive… front-line… Clubcall service for… Leeds… United… Football… Club.

"Listen to… Clubcall… for all the latest… news… and… information…"

Because we were paying by the second.

The War of the Roses

and the battle of the beech tree
outside Hillsborough, 1977

XMAS MORNING

Our 1970s Christmases, in our terrace front rooms and boxy housing-estate semis, weren't quite the same as the sumptuous Victorian festivals portrayed on Christmas cards and chocolate boxes, in TV ads and cartoons.

We didn't have stockings hanging from huge holly-bedecked fireplaces. We had striped pillowcases stuck on the end of our beds.

We didn't have gaily laughing guests – gentlemen in top hats and ladies wearing furry muffs – we had bald men round in their new V-neck jumpers, and they hardly spoke.

And we had, to be frank, shite artificial Christmas trees, not those towering, richly decorated spruces portrayed on the cover of the *Radio Times*.

As for the romantic notion of a White Christmas, it never snowed round our way; though sometimes it rained.

Christmas dinner was the same as normal Sunday dinner, except with turkey instead of roast beef, and with added parsnips and sprouts. Rather than the mouthwatering spreads portrayed ... well, you get the idea.

But somehow, on Christmas morning, with Noel Edmonds visiting children in hospital as a televisual backdrop, we still managed to reach a goosebump-inducing level of excitement.

"Billy Bremner was the best Buttons I've ever seen. **He came skipping down the aisle throwing out sweets to the kids. He was a natural, Billy.**"

Jimmy Armfield

And it was all because we knew that, concealed in cheap Woolies wrapping paper, piled up under the shite tree, there lurked *Shoot!* annuals, Wembley Trophy footballs, full football strips and Subbuteo accessories housed in their pale green boxes.

So we never took a horse-drawn sled down to the pine forest to chop down the tallest tree to place by the main staircase like those privileged Victorians... but then, they never had Subbuteo Team No. 21: Leeds United/Real Madrid, did they?

And they certainly didn't get the chance to go to one of the infamous Leeds United Christmas pantomimes at the City Varieties Music Hall, with Billy Bremner as Buttons, Norman Hunter as Prince Charming... and Duncan McKenzie as Cinderella.

THE VIDEO AGE

The VHS videocassette: like a DVD printed out on a long strand of tinsel.

Seldom has a new technology flared so brightly and died so quickly as video.

The race to develop a consumer-level video system was run in 1970s Japan, with JVC and their VHS eventually managing to overshadow Sony's Betamax system, and by 1978 the first video players were available in the UK. Available, but far from affordable for all but the spoilt kids.

Most families got one some time in the middle of the Eighties. It's pretty easy to work out because that's when our magpie collections of *Match of the Day* on Kodak E-180 tapes begins – not forgetting *Saint & Greavsie* and *Football Focus* editions snagged for posterity, when the ability to capture moving pictures off the telly box still seemed like something out of *Buck Rogers in the 25th Century*.

Whether painstakingly taping goals from the regional news, or building up a video library that could be measured in yards, it was an obsessive, and ultimately a pitifully pointless exercise.

No one now plays their rare early white-label editions of black-and-white match footage from the Whites' successes in the Sixties, never mind Danny Baker's *Own Goals and Gaffs* and the endless run of season highlights from seasons that somehow now seem to all run together in the mind. They're all out in the garage now, along with the precious unplayed vinyl and the music cassettes and the slideshow projector and the magic vegetable peeler gimmicks, still mint and boxed up the same as the day you bought them from the stall on the market.

One day, the plan is to get a special machine where you link it up to your computer and convert them all into DVDs. One day.

Gary Edwards on the Kop back in the day, when he only hadn't missed a single match for 10 years!

THE FAN WHO HASN'T MISSED A MATCH SINCE 1968...

Gary Edwards (seen here in the Kop at Elland Road in the 1970s) has not missed a single competitive Leeds United match since January 1968. He's only missed one friendly (not his fault!), which includes anywhere in the world Leeds have played. It's an incredible nigh-on 50-year adventure, which is going to be played out in full, in a new book to be released in May 2014, written by Gary himself along with Andy Starmore.

Gary with number one *Got, Not Got; Leeds* contributor Andy Starmore... and Finchy out of *The Office!*

The book will be following his exploits to every single ground that Leeds have played in Britain and Europe since Gary's first of the consecutive matches at Derby County. From tragedy in Birmingham and Istanbul to escaping a police compound in Nottingham – from behind the Iron Curtain to an eerie Nou Camp – from pink faces in Barnsley to disguises at Luton – Gary's stories will make you wince, they'll make you gasp but, above all, they'll make you laugh.

Not that this is a good thing, kids, but he even escaped school to travel abroad simply to follow Leeds!

Gary with our other number one *Got, Not Got; Leeds* contributor Neil Jeffries, and Andy's son Ben Starmore.

Authors

Gary Silke and Derek Hammond are the authors of *The Lost World of Football* (Pitch, 2013); *What A Shot! Your Snaps of the Lost World of Football* (Pitch, 2013), and *Got, Not Got: The A-Z of Lost Football Culture, Treasures & Pleasures* (Pitch, 2011).

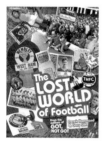  

Picture Credits

Neville Chadwick Photography: Front cover, 56, 75, 82, 90, 97, 98, 103. 110, 132, 136.
Getty Images: 10, 12, 20, 24, 28, 52, 62, 78, 83, 84, 107, 122, 134.
Andy Starmore: 8, 36, 44, 70, 74, 104, 116, 118, 119, 126, 128, 130, 140.
Vectis Auctions – collectible toy specialists, vectis.co.uk: 58 (ice cream van), 95 (boxed Mettoy Bremner figure).
Mike Schorah: 65, 94.

Acknowledgments

Grateful thanks to Andy Starmore and Neil Jeffries for so many of the images of Leeds United memorabilia in this book.

And to Jonathon Wheatley, whose luscious matchworn Admiral shirt collection can be viewed at freewebs.com/weedosenglandgear.

Further thanks to Paul Woozley, the proprietor of the excellent oldfootballgames. co.uk website, who let us take photos of, and even play with, all his great stuff.

Nigel Mercer for his jam-jar lids, *Lion* league ladders and Letraset. Check out his ace, encyclopaedic football card and sticker website at cards.littleoak.com.au. And, if you're a Letraset fan, the SPLAT Archives at action-transfers.com.

Andy Ormerod for his Sun Soccerstamps album.

And good luck to Gary and Andy with the book!

More Critical Acclaim for *Got, Not Got*

"This exquisite book is a homage to the game of 40 years ago – not just the mudheaps and the mavericks but a celebration of its wider culture [which] rises above lazy, modern-life-is-rubbish nostalgia... The design is so sumptuous and the stories so well chosen and written that it's hard to resist the authors' conclusion that much – call it charm, character or even romance – has been lost in the rush for cash. Regardless of whether it really was a golden age, this is a golden volume, as much a social history as a sports book. If you've not got *Got, Not Got*, you've got to get it."
Backpass

"I can guarantee that virtually anybody who flicks open this magnificent book will immediately want to have it."
The Football Trader

"For further reminders of the long-lost game of the 1960s, '70s and '80s, the illuminating new book *Got, Not Got* does a very fine job."
Sport magazine

"If, like myself, you are an unashamed nostalgia junkie, this book is for you. It's more than just a book on football collectables, including memories and experiences from the golden age – a time before the FA Premiership and TV money took us through a pound-sign portal and into a parallel, but much less likeable, universe. Some of my favourite experiences/memories are included – I found myself saying either 'did it' or 'remember it' – and there's a heck of a lot to choose from."
Programme Monthly

"A huge success and an epic tome for lovers of football nostalgia everywhere."
The Football Attic blog

"It's an absolute beauty."
Adrian Goldberg, BBC Radio WM.

"An absolute gem of a book – part brilliantly written lament for an earlier age, part opportunity to reminisce about a time when you hankered after a Garden Goal ('Every Boy's Dream!')... Football's relentless commercialisation comes, naturally enough, at a cost. It's brought us everything from the Stalinist-style obliteration of the game's pre-1992 history to the modern player, kissing the badge, logo and sponsor's name after scoring. A purer, less cynical era is depicted throughout *Got, Not Got*. Buy it – you will not be disappointed."
SportsBookoftheMonth.com

"The best dose of retro football nostalgia ever. I can't put it down!"
footballcardsuk.com

"It's a beautiful book – a smorgasbord!"
John Keith, City Talk FM, Liverpool

"An exhaustively researched collection of football programmes, stickers, badges and memorabilia, a coffee table book you can dip in and out of at any time. Some of the advertisements from old programmes are classics – 'Bovril – hot favourite for the cup!' Or culinary advice to players: 'Full English – eat up your fried bread now, it's full of energy.' Eat your heart out Arsene Wenger."
Christopher Davies, Football Writers Association Book Reviews, footballwriters.co.uk